Knight Rose Press

knightrosepress.com
Trumansburg, NY, USA

Copyright © 2021 by Scott Dawson

ISBN
978-1-7339913-3-9

Library of Congress Control Number
2021923424

For Amy, Elizabeth, and Xander

Foreword

I'm a remote work veteran, having worked from a home office since 1998. I could not have foreseen the coronavirus pandemic's impact on the world of remote work. It upended entire industries, thrusting us into situations we never thought we'd be in. We didn't commute on trains, planes, or buses. Instead, we traversed hallways and staircases in our homes, townhouses, and apartments. We didn't settle into desks in corner offices with expansive city views. We occupied kitchen table corners and jockeyed for the best views of the outside world. We didn't have the clear boundaries of a necessary commute to bookend our day. We were stuck in a never-ending loop of work, life, and sleep. We didn't enjoy geographical or temporal markers to guide our day. For some of us, it was a genuine struggle. For others, it was just another day in the office.

Scott Dawson

I wrote The Art of Working Remotely in 2018 and 2019. It went on sale in July 2019, just six months shy of the start of the pandemic. When the lockdowns began, my entire team started working 100% remotely. We'd been a hybrid team until then, so we were well-positioned to continue thriving. Others were not as fortunate. The struggle was real, and so many of the reasons I wrote the book snapped into acute focus. I heard from people all over the world about how much it helped them. I saw an uptick of interest in #RemoteChat, the weekly community-oriented chat I moderated on Twitter from 2016 through 2021.

The world of remote work-related advice became cacophonous. It was difficult to cut through the chatter: everyone shared prescriptive advice in books, articles, and podcasts. Problem is, a lot of that prescriptive advice skimmed the surface and never dove deeply to the root of the matter. We've all read the same boilerplate "how to work from home" blog posts. They all recommend the exact same things.

In a Twitter post, I pointedly asked, When will "working remotely" simply become "working?" I've felt this way for a long time, but eagerly anticipate a working world where geography is generally not a distinction. If the pull of some companies back to office life is a sign, the answer is a resounding 'not yet.' One thing is clear, though. Remote work is here to stay, even more so as a result of the pandemic.

On January 1, 2021, I set a goal to write 365 practical and unique tips about thriving as a distributed worker. Here's what I wrote on that day.

I'll be publishing a helpful work or life-related tip every day in 2021. By the end of the year, it should be rather impressive to look back at 365 (hopefully inspiring) pieces of advice. They'll be related in some way to success at work or life, with a distinct leaning toward thriving in a distributed workplace. The very first one is directly related to this goal. It's all about taking that first, crucial step, no matter your goal.

I posted tips on Twitter and LinkedIn every day. Before January was up, I doubled my cadence: for every daily tip I wrote, I wrote one for later in the year. Some tips are from my book and others are new, garnered from my own experiences over the last few years. The tips will help you level up your working game, regardless of where, when, or how you do it. On July 19, my list met in the middle of my spreadsheet. Mission accomplished!

I sat back and reveled in my achievement. Three hundred sixty-five is a lot of anything, and to see them all in once place? Wow. I knew then what I had to do. The tips I wrote cover the entire range of concerns for anyone not working in a traditional office environment. Communication, discipline, health, performance, managing up, managing others, leading meetings, professional development, quality workspaces, and networking. As a compendium, they'd be a fantastic resource for anyone working in this modern world. And now you hold it in your hand. A literal handbook for the modern worker.

Who's *that*, anyway? The *modern worker* isn't a popular term at the moment when it comes to describing remote work, distributed work, or hybrid teams ... but it should be. The workplace is always in flux. Technology evolves. Teams change. Industries adapt. We communicate asynchronously. Workforces can be entirely virtual, or hybrid with some together, some apart. The world seems smaller and larger, all at the same time. And as the pandemic showed us, geography doesn't have to dictate how we get work done. We all play in this constantly evolving sandbox, and that makes us modern workers.

Who knows what the working world will look like in the next decade or two? Nobody, really. But if you keep these tips front of mind, your career will be, as a good friend of mine says, 'rich and full.'

I hope you enjoy the read, whether you rip through it in a few sittings, patiently go through it day-by-day, or randomly open it up when you need some inspiration. If you want to get in touch, find me @scottpdawson or scottpdawson.com.

Scott Dawson
December 2021

1.

Don't let the size of an endeavor overwhelm you. Just take the first step.

Whether it's a personal or professional goal, the toughest step can be the first one you take. Make a plan, gather your resources, and take that step. Momentum will follow.

2.

Master your reaction to change.

Change is the one thing you can count on in this life. You can embrace it, tactfully challenge it, or remain unaffected by it. It's your choice.

3.

Don't just grease the squeaky wheels.

Spend time with everyone in your circle, not only the "squeaky wheels." You may get reinforcement of the things that are going well, but you might find out something new, too. You'll be a better manager for asking, and you'll paint a more comprehensive picture of your team.

4.

Don't burn bridges. Instead, preserve pathways.

Troubled by an interaction with a boss, colleague, or someone else? You never know where, when, or how your paths will cross again. Upset by something in the moment? Step away, disconnect, and return when calmer heads prevail.

5.

Invest in your workspace.

You'll spend a ton of time in your remote workspace. Any investment — in making it more ergonomic, pleasant, or comfortable — is a smart one.

6.

Be inquisitive.

Ah, curiosity. All the facts are rarely on the table from the outset, so ask relevant "why" questions until you get them. Being informed can help you make better decisions.

7.

If at first you don't succeed, try another angle.

Ah, the collision of two adages. It's said that the definition of insanity is repeating the same steps and expecting a different result. It's also said that practice makes perfect. Sometimes, though, the path to success lies in traversing another path. Try approaching the problem from a different angle. Step away, evaluate your approach, adjust your plan, and try again.

8.

Make time to take stock.

Need to demonstrate your effectiveness to someone, even if that's just you? Take stock of your accomplishments at a set interval: the end of the workweek is as good a time as any. Set a recurring reminder in your calendar and document the important things. The more quantifiable, the better. Do you have a formal review at the end of the year? Good. Your documentation will be invaluable as you paint a comprehensive picture of your work.

9.

Color outside the lines.

You may have heard advice like "stay in your lane" or "stick to your knitting." Specialization can make you a star, depending on where you are. However, consider exploring areas peripheral or unrelated to your core mission. You might learn something that, when combined with your core work, creates a novel and magical thing. Go make magic.

10.

Write well.

Most remote work interactions are virtual. Consider the importance and persistence of written communication: emails, instant messaging, documentation, status updates, and texting. People will judge you based on the quality of your communication. When you write something, write it well.

11.

Have more than a hunch about your lunch.

You take a break in the middle of your workday to eat, right? Be intentional about your plan and you'll be less likely to unhealthily improvise. Try to prepare your lunch in advance. Microwave heating is fair game, but Crock-Pot makes fantastic personal-sized warmers, too. There's nothing better than piping hot food whenever you're ready for it.

12.

Tame your administrivia.

Ah, administrivia. Trivial tasks (emails, bill paying, cleaning, and social media) can consume swaths of your schedule if you let them. Put together a strategy for tackling administrivia without sacrificing workday productivity. One tried-and-true method: chunk up each type of task and do them all at once. You can batch tasks daily at a specific time, weekly, or on some other sensible schedule.

13.

Cultivate your background.

When you're on video, be aware of what your background says about you. It's your chance to express your personality, but make it an appropriate expression. Art, photos, books, plants, or other personal effects are all fair game. Piles of bills, laundry, or clutter are not. If you must use a virtual background in a bid to hide clutter, go for it. However, be aware of their potential to distract others and hamper authenticity.

14.

Give the gift of time.

Think about how you can best save others' time. Before you schedule a meeting, ask: can I do the same thing asynchronously? If you are meeting, before requiring someone's attendance, ask: are they required? Give them the option to attend, and be ready to accept it if they don't.

15.

Speak up.

See something you think can be improved?
Speak up. Witness a wrong that should be
righted? Speak up. Need something, like
training or tools, to make your work life
easier? Speak up. You may not get the
response you're hoping for, but speak up.
Silence is consent.

16.

Accept the things you cannot change.

This key clause of the serenity prayer can unblock so much of the angst that comes with an unpleasant situation. You may be stuck with a bad boss, a tough client, or an annoying colleague. If you accept the situation for what it is, at least for the moment, you can more readily take steps to make the situation more bearable.

17.

Know when to ask for help.

Sometimes, the Internet can't help you and you need to ask someone for help. That's okay! People like to help, especially if you've tried everything you can and are still stuck. Write down what you've tried, which in itself may reveal the answer. Then, ask away.

18.

When helping someone, teach them.

It's worth the extra time and effort to not only answer a question or solve a problem but to help teach along the way. What you're teaching may be useful to many people! Take the time to share as broadly as is appropriate: a Wiki update, blog post, or an update on social. Sharing is caring!

19.

If you're feeling sick, recuperate and rest.

Think working from home excuses you from taking time to recuperate? Think again. You might choose to work at times you feel subpar, and that's okay. Know where the line is, though. If you feel sick enough, take time to recuperate. Rest. Don't check your email. Don't take calls. And don't apologize for taking care of yourself.

20.

Seek out new challenges.

Seek out new challenges to open professional pathways. You might be able to do this as part of your normal workday or invest non-work time. Express interest in a new project. Try out new technologies or skills with online or in-person learning. It's a simple cause-and-effect: when you challenge yourself, you grow.

21.

Counter the 'out of sight, out of mind' mentality.

When you're not physically with others on your team, or with your manager, you need to be very intentional about communicating your impact. In a distributed meeting? Great. Contribute, ask questions, and speak up. Did you receive a compliment about your work from someone outside your group? Share it. Does your team use a collaboration platform? Be active, proactive, and helpful there.

22.

Adore your door.

One of the most important items in your remote work arsenal pivots on a trio of hinges. You can shut a door when you need privacy for an important meeting. A door signals to others that you're busy. A door can dampen noise coming from other rooms where you're working. If you have the luxury of a workspace with a door, you're in good shape.

23.

Be tactfully candid.

Business is about relationships. In relationships, candor is key. If you have something to say, don't beat around the bush and hope that your message will land. This is especially important when you have something difficult to communicate. It's never a license to be rude or caustic, though. Balance your openness and honesty with tact and sensitivity.

24.

Get lost to
get going again.

You know that moment when you're totally
stuck and don't know how to proceed? It's
frustrating. Get up and go for a midday run,
walk, or hike. Do something other than work.
You may come up with the solution to your
problem in the first 10 minutes. It's a wise
investment of time, especially if it gets you
going again.

25.

Set your own bar for success.

You probably know how "society" views success in your field. What does success mean to you, though? When you define your own success criteria, you'll do it in terms that are important to you. Those terms may not be all about money, promotion, or notoriety. But they'll be 100% tailored to you, and that's a bar worth hitting.

26.

Find the work that brings you joy.

Joy is defined as "a feeling of great pleasure and happiness." Do you always correlate your workday with pleasure and happiness? Great! But if you're stuck in a joyless job, take stock of where you're at in your career. It might be time for a change. Refine your goals, do some professional development, or reboot into a different industry.

27.

Set a daily goal for physical activity.

Regular physical activity can be so important to your health. It can help your concentration, memory, and creativity. Does anyone out there want to lower their stress level? Exercise does that, too. Make personal fitness a priority and incorporate it into your day. Take a brisk walk before work. Go for a run or hike between appointments. Do some weight training before dinner, or yoga before bed. Planning in advance will help you keep accountable.

28.

Make tough decisions and own them.

Faced with a tough decision? Make it and own it. If you try to avoid the discomfort or inconvenience of a large impactful decision by making smaller ones instead, you may fail. It's far better to make the tough call and solve a problem instead of applying band-aids you hope will help.

29.

Know when to call it a day.

One of the oft-cited drawbacks of working remotely is having blurry boundaries. Define an end to your workday so you can do other things that fulfill you before the next workday begins. That project or task that you're leaving unfinished? It'll be waiting for you tomorrow.

30.

Judiciously go into overtime.

One of the benefits of working remotely is the ability to put in extra effort when it's needed. Are you on a deadline? Attending to some kind of work-related emergency? Trying to wrap up something you know you can't leave undone? It can pay great dividends to invest non-work time to get it done. Flexibility goes both ways.

31.

Do what you do best.

Don't settle for a job that has you doing
something you're either not good at, or not
enthusiastic about. When you can leverage
your strengths, you'll be far happier and
productive. If you're a remote manager, get to
know your team members and their
strengths. Help them use those strengths
daily.

32.

Park yourself in all the best spaces.

Where do you sit or stand when you work? One of the benefits of distributed work is that you don't always have to work in the same space. You will find, however, that you spend most of your time in one area. Consider the view outside, your desk and chair, lighting, wall colors, and what you surround yourself with. Create a space that delights you!

33.

Take it one step at a time.

Do you ever get overwhelmed by the sheer enormity of a task? Break it down into smaller bits, so each one seems manageable. When you plan down to this level, you'll be far more comfortable with your ability to make steady progress. Marathons aren't completed in an instant; they're completed one step at a time.

34.

The best team offense is a solid management defense.

You hired the right people, gave them the right tools, and set solid success parameters, right? As a manager, shield your team from the noises and distractions that can derail them. Your defense in favor of their productivity is a fantastic strategy for success.

35.

Pronounce names properly.

We live and work in an international, intergenerational world. Names can be unique and sometimes it's not obvious how to pronounce them. Learn how. Listen to them introduce themselves to you or others, or ask them how to pronounce their name.

36.

Be disciplined.

When you're working in a shared space with others, discipline can come more easily because of the inherent oversight. When you're alone, you alone are responsible for getting your work done. You're in control. If you are distractible or tend to procrastinate, find ways to inject discipline into your day. One surefire method: make a plan and share it with others who will hold you accountable.

37.

Transcend your title.

Let's say you're in charge of producing widgets. Day in, day out, that's what you do. But one day, you have an idea to improve the design of the widgets. You tell yourself, "You're a producer, not a designer." And your idea dies right there. Transcend your title and let it live. Share it with those who need to hear it. It may go nowhere, or it may result in an evolutionary change for you. You won't know unless you share.

38.

Solicit input to gain perspective.

You don't have all the answers. You don't!
But, you can get them. When you have a
tough problem to solve, talk to others who
know what you need to know. When you get
perspective and background from others,
you'll have far more context. Draw on that
context when you moderate a meeting,
propose a solution, or weigh in with your
own thoughts.

39.

It's not about heroics.

If you rely on heroics to get your job done, you're doing it wrong. Do you rely on star performers? Burn the candle at both ends? Ask your team to do more with less? Heroics are not a sustainable business strategy. If you feel like you're the hero, remember that success is bigger than yourself. Success takes healthy relationships, strategic partnerships, and effective communication. Put your focus there and you'll all grow together.

40.

If you don't know, say so.

When put on the spot to answer a question, don't hem and haw. You either know the answer or you don't. "I think so" is a horrible hedge: it hints at a certain amount of confidence but leaves a huge amount of room for doubt. Don't guess. Be sure. If you're not, defer to someone who is.

41.

Seek understanding publicly.

If you don't understand something, it can be incredibly powerful to ask for more information in public. If you're in a meeting, get clarification in the moment. If you have a question, someone else in the group likely has the same exact question you do but is afraid to ask it. Same goes for online forums: one of the superpowers of the Internet is that people ask questions publicly, and the answers are there for all to see.

42.

Be a lifelong learner.

Do you know the difference between a fixed mindset and a growth mindset? Read about it and you'll believe in the concept of lifelong learning. Whether it's a job skill or a new hobby, learning something new can help keep the spark in your life. I've never learned a skill that I wasn't able to apply in some way, at work or play.

43.

Give credit where credit is due.

Did someone help you get where you are right now? Maybe you're sharing work your team has done by giving a demo, sending an email, or doing a webinar. Share details about who contributed: people love to get credit for their contributions. Better yet, if there's a chance (and willingness) for someone to share their own work, make room for that to happen.

44.

Be punctual.

It's a virtual world. You're either present or absent in a meeting. There's no such thing as 'they're almost here, they're in the hallway.' So, be on time for meetings that you're participating in. Moderating a meeting? Be a few minutes early. Doing a demo or a presentation to a large group? Be ready five to ten minutes early. Going to be late? Let someone know.

45.

Lead with compassion.

Kindness goes farther than you think. When you're virtual, it's harder to pick up on the non-verbals that can clue you into a larger problem. Someone may be having a tough time at work, enduring personal relationship stress, or struggling in another way. Imbue interactions with kindness and compassion. You'll create a stronger platform for healing. Turn that lens inward, too. You know when you need compassion yourself and you're the first person who can deliver the goods.

46.

Make time to celebrate.

It can be easy to let major milestones slip by.
Do you glance in the rear-view mirror to
pause and reflect on what led you there?
When you achieve a significant goal, take
time to celebrate your accomplishment. It
may be as simple as a half-hour virtual
gathering. Talk about what worked, what
could have gone better, and toast your
success. You and your team will come away
with a solid appreciation of the work you did,
and how it led to your accomplishment.

47.

Cast yourself in the best light.

If you are on video calls for any part of your workday, optimize your workspace to provide flattering light. Natural light is best, but don't sit facing away from the source. Natural light should be coming from in front of you or off to the side. If you need light sources in the room to illuminate your face better, position them in front of you in a range no greater than 45° from where you're facing. Place your camera at eye level. It's an easier angle to have a more natural interaction with others on the call.

48.

Get by with a little help from your friends.

Working remotely is likely a solitary activity. It doesn't mean you have to go it alone, though. You may be uncertain about something and need counsel. You may feel isolated and need companionship. You may have great news and want to share it. Whatever it is, don't keep it to yourself. Nobody goes very far when they're traveling alone. We can all get by with a little help from our friends.

49.

Compartmentalize.

You probably don't have a commute to serve as a barrier between your mornings and work, or work and your evenings. When you transition immediately to or from work, stressors can bleed from one into the other. Compartmentalization can help ease mental stress, but it can be hard to put into practice. Off the clock? Don't check work email. Hard at work? Save your personal correspondence for later. Put systems in place at work: task lists, ample documentation, and proper planning. These systems can free your mind and help you enjoy time with friends and family during non-work time.

50.

Embrace the crazy days.

Some days are laid back. Others, crazy. The latter can feel overwhelming and unsustainable, but they're where the magic happens. When you're performing well and not letting the crazy overwhelm you, you're nailing it. Frenetic might not be fun when it's happening, though, so remember that the less crazy days will return. Yeah, it's that 'change' thing. You can count on it!

51.

Bring humanity into the workplace.

Don't you love to learn more about who your coworkers are when they're not actively working? So much of in-office interaction is around our passions, our hobbies, and our families. When you're distributed, it should be no different. Show off your family, talk about your weekend plans, and share pictures and anecdotes. And what if someone else in your household makes an unplanned appearance on your video call? Don't stress about it. That's humanity, and that's definitely in bounds.

52.

Give yourself a break.

It's taxing to sit all day long at your desk. In a normal office environment, you get up to walk to the conference room, to the break room, or leave to go to a coffee shop. Give yourself the same treatment and build in breaks throughout the day. It may be as simple as a 20-minute walk or a coffee date with a friend you've been meaning to catch up with. Schedule these breaks: put them in your calendar. Step away, do something else, and come back refreshed.

53.

Plan to keep your nutrition in check.

Tempting snacks can be as close and available as you want them to be when you're working from home. Don't let the proximity of your fridge and pantry derail your day. Plan ahead to help keep your nutrition in check. What will you have for lunch? What will your snacks be? When will you eat them? Knowing this can help prevent grazing when stress comes knocking on your door.

54.

Systematize your day.

You can tame a lot of the noise in your day with systems. The modern worker can use synchronized lists, task managers, cloud-based documents and spreadsheets, and automation. Most services have free tiers that are entirely adequate. Take a close look at what consumes your time. Can you batch tasks, create shared lists, or automate something that's tedious? Systematize and reap the productivity benefits.

55.

Become a pro at task management.

You might not have total discretion over which task management tool to use for your job. If you do, though, do your homework. Find a solution that works for you (that may not be a software solution) and stick with it. Don't waste time looking for something better unless it's been at least a few years and you find yourself craving functionality that's not there. Invest time in becoming a proficient user. You'll gain time and increase productivity when you wield your tools and techniques like a pro.

56.

Make time to connect.

It can be tempting to let each day slip by, keep your head down, and do good work. That's only part of the recipe for success, though. If you're on a team, either as a manager or individual contributor, make time to connect with those around you. Getting the team together can help share common values and goals. Getting together one-on-one can reveal opportunities for improvement, or reinforce good habits. Meeting with senior leadership can give you exposure and recognition. Find a frequency that works for all, schedule it, and help foster connection.

57.

Bid adieu to vices and video games.

Negative addictions have no place in your nine-to-five. It's your choice to have them in your non-work time, though. Addicted to the latest binge-worthy show on a streaming service? Can't stop playing the game that's engineered to keep you playing for hours? You'll be more productive and happier if you can't access these addictions. Put up a firewall, use parental controls for yourself, or delete that addictive app.

58.

Bring some weekend into your weekday.

You know that feeling when you've been at it for a little too long? It's harder to focus and frustration comes to the fore far sooner than it should. Take some breaks between sprints of work to maximize your mental fitness. Meditation, stretching, exercise, a light chore, or a short show can recenter you when you need it. These breaks are an abbreviated version of that far bigger break you should also take: the weekend.

59.

Don't leave chores to chance.

I know, not everyone is champing at the bit to do chores all day long. If they're in your line of sight, though, you might be tempted to tackle them during your workday. That can be disruptive. Laundry. Dishes. Floors. Cleaning. Groceries. Group a few of these together and you won't get any work done! The solution is simple: set up a schedule. Each task will have a designated day, so you can take comfort that everything will get done. Just not all today.

60.

Learn to say no.

No. It's a short word, but it can be difficult or impossible to say. If you don't feel comfortable with something, or you don't have the time for it, say no. This applies to all things personal or professional and requests large or small. Say no. There are plenty of guides that'll help you do this politely, without being rude, and without guilt. Search for "how to say no" to get started.

61.

Are you busy or are you free?

Do you work in the same place as other people? Communication can be one of the best tools to create an ideal, quiet work environment. Tell others if you're giving an important presentation or attending a critical meeting. You'll be grateful for the quiet when the time comes. Signs on your home office door are a great way to let others know when you're busy and free, too. Door hangers, electronic signs, or simple handwritten notes can help communicate your status.

62.

Dress to impress.

Sure, if you have a meeting where you want to look your very best, do so. On normal days, dress to impress upon yourself the importance and value of work. When you start work wearing what you slept in, you signal the opposite to yourself. You don't have to go all-out with your wardrobe, but be intentional about getting dressed. Ditch the comfortable pajamas and put on something you'd be proud to leave your house in. You'll be camera-ready and your mind will know it's time to work.

63.

Lend context to your correspondence.

Quick, think of the worst way to start a virtual chat. You might think of 'Hey', or 'Are you free?', or 'Got a sec?', or the perhaps-sinister 'We need to talk.' Lack of context can induce anxiety, especially if the chat is between a supervisor and an employee. Add some context like this: "Hey, you have a sec to talk about the contract issues?" The recipient now knows what you want to talk about. That'll help them decide if they're prepared (or have time) to continue the conversation.

64.

You won't regret an office pet.

Sharing an office with a pet can be wonderful for all parties involved. It's nice to have a constant companion during weekdays. A pet can smooth out the stressful highs and emotional lows of your workday and improve your morale. It's great for your pet, too. It's comforting for them to be in a shared space with another human. Pets are great icebreakers, too, even if you're virtual. It's easy to start a conversation when an animal enters the picture.

65.

Master the business of being social.

How well do you know the other people you work with? When you interact only around work, you miss part of the picture. Schedule a recurring agenda-free time to meet as a group. Give yourself a space to be with others without a specific business problem to solve or status to update. You'll get to know each other so much better! This closer connection, in turn, will help ease business-oriented interactions.

66.

Ruthlessly edit yourself.

Context, clarity, and brevity are three hallmarks of effective communication. When you're writing or speaking, ask yourself: can this be shorter, yet still as clear? Think about what you need to communicate before you commit to your message. Start with an outline if that makes sense. Context: am I giving enough information for the recipient to know what I'm talking about? Clarity: is what I'm communicating as clear as it can be? Brevity: am I being direct? Once you have your message, ruthlessly edit it once more.

67.

Don't underestimate the power of positive thinking.

Who has control over what you think about? You do, of course! Who obsesses over failing a test, freezing during a presentation, or flubbing a pitch? When you think something bad might happen you might increase the chances it happens. When you think of a positive outcome and imagine your success, you may edge the odds in your favor. Your emotional and mental attitude is all up to you. Think positive and see what happens! **Editor's Note:** I wrote about my experience with positive thinking as a youth*. The ordeal helped me harness mental toughness, have a positive attitude, and practice positive self-talk.

* scottpdawson.com/positive-mental-attitude-the-service-of-pma-the-moose

68.

Be kind to everyone.

Conditional kindness: you know it when you see it. Someone is kind only when they need something. Someone is pleasant with their superiors while they abuse subordinates. Someone is sweet-as-pie with their friends but caustic with service workers. What goes around comes around. You don't know what others are going through. Will your paths will cross in different circumstances? Be kind to everyone, if only because it's the right thing to do.

69.

Work in your window.

No, silly. Not your literal window. That might be dangerous! You know when you're most productive. You might be a morning person or an evening person. The concept of flex time can be easily adopted when you're working on a distributed team. Bonus points if your team communicates asynchronously across time zones. Identify when you're most productive and try your best to safeguard that time for deep work. You don't necessarily have to stick to the 9-5 schedule if you prefer starting at 6 a.m. or finishing at 11 p.m.

70.

Tell the story you want to be heard.

March 11*, or 311, has me thinking about how we portray ourselves online. After all, 311 is a non-emergency phone number you can call in many big cities to get information. Online channels are the primary way others can learn about you. What do they see? It's worth the time to think about your personal brand. How does that come through in your personal website, what you write about, or how you appear on social media? You don't have to play in all these sandboxes, but if you do, make sure the story that's told is the one you want to be heard.

This tip was originally published on March 11, 2021

71.

Share how you feel.

It may be tempting to always have your game
face on at work. However, it's good to share
how you're feeling, even if the only byproduct
is your own unburdening. It's more likely,
though, that you find out you're not alone.
Sharing can help unearth trends in how a
team is doing. Sharing can help bring more
empathy into the workplace. Sharing can lead
to change. These can all lead to greater
satisfaction and productivity at work.

72.

Practice makes you better.

Did you learn something new and want to excel at it? Practice. Don't have a chance to do it yet at your day job? Take nights and weekends time to learn, practice, and refine your craft. Promise yourself you'll do it. Every day that passes with inaction creates a higher barrier to surmount. Exercise discipline and your efforts will pay off. You'll get to apply it on the job or launch yourself in a new, better direction.

73.

When it comes to tech, trust but verify.

Technology is great. Most of the time, it does what it's advertised to without tiring or complaining. That said, verify that it does what you expect before you need it. If you need to deliver a presentation using features you've not yet tried, test it out in advance. Dry runs are your friend. Learn how things work in advance and remember what you experience. When you're under pressure in the moment, the learnings from your dry run will be invaluable.

74.

Talk to yourself.

Are you stuck on a problem? Would you normally reach out to a colleague for help? Try talking to yourself first. Speak through what you know, what's not working, and what you've tried. This act can help spark connections in your brain. When you put thoughts into words, you implicitly analyze the problem and put things in the proper order. As you talk to yourself, listen for the answers. You just might find them.

75.

Schedule with sensitivity.

It's a global world. More and more business is being done asynchronously. If you must have a meeting, though, be sensitive as you craft your invitation list. Find a day and time that respects the boundaries people may have set for themselves. Not too early. Not too late. Be aware of time zones. Also, only invite those who are necessary. There's nothing worse than finding yourself in a meeting you can't contribute to.

76.

Knowledge is power.

Siloed information only benefits the owner of that information. If you find something useful, chances are others will, too. Procedural knowledge can help others follow steps to an intended outcome. Contextual information can help someone understand why what they're doing is important. Share and persist information: email is okay, but a wiki or online knowledge base is so much better. Make it clear, concise, and findable. Your future self, and your fellow workers, will appreciate it.

77.

Ignorance is bliss.

This is the perfect corollary to the prior tip. Avoid sharing when your team is focused. You'll only add to the noise and distract them. There's a time and place for sharing information. If you get it wrong you'll frustrate your intended audience. Share when you need to share. When the tactical importance of what you need to share isn't clear, save it for another time. Don't be a distraction.

78.

Expect the unexpected.

When you have rigid expectations, you can
be sure they'll be unmet. At the end of an
ordinary week, think back to the beginning of
the week. Did the outcome align with your
expectations? Likely not. When you're flexible
about your expectations, you won't be
disappointed when they're not met. Expect
the unexpected. Timelines can shift. Tasks
can take longer than planned. Business deals
can sour. Adjust your expectations and the
unexpected might happen a little less often.

79.

Put a plan in place to combat loneliness.

Loneliness is one of the most often-cited drawbacks of working on your own. Identifying that emotion and sharing how you feel, first with yourself, is an essential first step to countering it. Put a plan in place to combat loneliness: don't wait for others to get in touch with you. Get in touch with them: propose a coffee, walk, hike, or a virtual gathering. Don't despair if it doesn't work out the first time you ask. People can be busy. Try again and be politely persistent in your pursuit of fellowship.

80.

Set ambitious goals.

Ambitious goal-setting is important any time of the year. Make sure they're realistic and measurable. Goals will help you assess your performance when it's time for reviews. They'll also keep you on a solid heading throughout the year. By stating a goal, you breathe life into it. By documenting it and charting a course, you give it hope. By visualizing and working toward it daily, you spur it into existence.

81.

Async video can be powerful.

Video can be a great way to asynchronously convey complex ideas to a distributed group. There are easy (and free) ways to record your screen with audio on both Apple and Microsoft platforms. Video works great for point-to-point communication, too. Don't send your colleague a lengthy email to explain something that's inherently visual. Capture it as a short video or animated gif and send it that way.

82.

Be transparent.

Lack of transparency is one reason managers might not be comfortable with remote work. They can't see you, so find ways to remove shreds of doubt about your productivity. You don't have to be a completely open book, mind you. If you proactively communicate your status, that'll help improve the situation.

83.

Daily routines combat stress.

Non-work activities can play a major role in managing your stress levels. Daily routines can help mitigate stressful feelings. Go for a walk every morning. Eat at similar times throughout the day. Set (and stick to) solid times to sleep and wake up. Find things that bring you joy and make a habit of doing them daily. You might find that a solid routine, morning to night, can blunt the effects of stress.

84.

Manage up.

If you don't directly manage anyone, you still have to "manage up." Visibility is so important for promotion, longevity, and satisfaction. How can you be visible when you're remote? You must advocate for yourself. Have an idea? Share it. Do something cool? Share it. Concerned about something? Share it. It's the only way to counter the "out of sight, out of mind" realities that remote work reinforces.

85.

Create physical boundaries.

When you work and live in the same space, the lines between the two modes can become concernedly blurry. Create routines around transitioning from one mode to the other. Do you have a dedicated space for work? It's effective to leave it at the end of the workday. Bonus points if that space has a door! If you're working in a shared space, stow your notes, phone, and laptop away when you're done for the day. Out of sight, out of mind!

86.

Don't present a choice if there really isn't one.

People love to have their opinions and feelings considered when a choice is being made. When you involve others in your analysis and decision-making, you give them a stake in the outcome and make them feel empowered. If you've already decided, though, don't give the impression that you'll consider their input. State your rationale, make the decision, and move on. Anything else will seem disingenuous.

87.

Cultivate a safe environment.

Are you struggling with emotions? Don't fear being vulnerable with others, including your direct supervisor. Sharing can help you start to overcome what you're struggling with. If you manage others, cultivate a safe environment where organic sharing can occur. It'll help you forge strong team bonds, especially if there's no fear that sharing will have an adverse effect on one's job.

88.

Green up your space.

Research shows that working alongside indoor plants conveys psychological and physical health benefits. It's true! We spend a ton of time indoors, and that has the unfortunate side effect of disconnecting us from nature. So, bring a little outside in by adding a small plant to your desk, a large plant in the corner, or something between. Your stress levels will thank you.

89.

Mix sitting and standing for optimal health.

How many hours do you sit each day? Sitting all day can be bad for your health, so find ways to stand throughout the day. Set a timer to remind yourself to get up every half hour to move around. Standing desks can help you adjust your position throughout the day, too. Taking meetings while walking (bonus points if it's nice outside) can be a great way to log non-sitting time.

90.

Remember there's a person behind every curtain.

Artificial intelligence doesn't run the world yet. Behind every process, you're likely to find a person. Whether it's resolving a support ticket, getting help with your hardware, or resolving a customer service issue, remember: there's someone like you on the other end. Imbue your interactions with a dose of empathy and understanding. You never know where or when your paths will cross again.

91.

Type faster.

No matter your industry, it's a good bet you spend a fair amount of your time typing on a keyboard. Learn to type faster. You'll gain efficiencies every time you write an email, author a document, or chat with a colleague. You'll get thoughts from your brain to the proverbial paper faster. When you're chatting synchronously, speed helps the conversation flow more freely. There are many free ways to improve your typing, so start by searching online for 'type faster.'

92.

Backup your work.

Think about the data that means the most to you. How redundant is it? Keep a local backup using an external hard drive. Then, add more redundancy with a cloud-based backup service you trust. When you have data redundancy, you'll be far less exposed when hardware fails (and it will).

93.

Be specific and timely when giving feedback.

When you give feedback to someone, give it as close as possible to the action that spurred the feedback. Don't wait for an infrequent time, like a semi-annual or annual performance review. Feedback is more valuable if the receiver can correlate it to something they did or didn't do. Be direct. Focus on specific things you observed, not on generalities like their attitude. Conclude your feedback by stating what you expect to see in the future. Lastly, avoid the feedback sandwich, where layers of praise obscure actual criticism.

94.

Deploy scents for your senses.

In the spirit of customizing your space, it's easy to think about what you can see or hear. But what about your sense of smell? It's one of the potential issues when working with others in shared spaces, but when you're on your own, you can use scents that make you happy. Think about scents that make you smile and use them. Diffusers, candles, or open windows to the outside world are all fair game.

95.

Take time to smell the roses.

If you have paid time off as a term of your employment, use it. If you're a solo practitioner, make the time to disconnect. When you feel the need to recharge throughout the year, do so. It might be a few days here and there or a solid stretch of weeks. Powering through with depleted energy seldom works out well and can lead to burnout. So, take the time to smell those roses. Your work will be waiting for you when you're done!

96.

Make contingency plans to connect.

What happens if your primary way of connecting with colleagues and clients fails? Will you be able to connect with others if your Internet goes out? What about your phone, or power? Think about redundancy and make contingency plans if they fail. You might tether to your phone if your Internet fails, or have a backup location to work if your home loses power. Store key work contact details in a few places. That'll be critical if your primary device with that contact information fails.

97.

Put yourself first.

Few things are worth putting yourself on the line for, and work is probably not one of them. When you're feeling stressed, burned out, or frazzled, ask yourself: am I putting myself first? When you prioritize your well-being, you give yourself the mental space to deal with the sources of stress. Make sure you're getting adequate sleep, exercise, and quality food. Everything else can wait.

98.

Relish in the big screen.

No, this isn't a tip about going to the movies. It's about monitors! The saying "go big or go home" is not quite right when you're talking about monitors. It should be "go big if you're working at home." Think about what your workspace and computer can support. Multiple monitors are great. Wide-screen or curved monitors might be in your price range, too. Once you enjoy having applications side-by-side with ample screen space, you won't willingly go back to smaller screens.

99.

Tackle your tough tasks first.

You might like to start your day with easier tasks. After all, who doesn't love to show a little progress? That said, you might enjoy things more if they become easier over time. If you tackle a tough task first and relegate easier work for later, you might enjoy the process more. Otherwise, you may defer or lower the priority of tough tasks in favor of smaller wins. If you have peak energy shortly after you start work, block off that time and commit to doing the tough tasks first.

100.

Record incremental progress.

Do you have a long-term goal you're trying to reach? It can be helpful to record and report on your incremental progress. Whether you keep tabs on hours, task completion, or another metric, seeing steady progress toward a long-term goal can be a great motivator. Metrics help you stay on track and give you the assurance you need to keep working.

101.

Keep an eye on your eyes.

We spent a lot of time looking at screens of all shapes and sizes. If you're feeling the effects of eye strain, check out the 20-20-20 rule. It's simple: for every 20 minutes of screen time, take a break to look at something at least 20 feet away for 20 seconds. Visit an optometrist yearly to check your vision and gauge the health of your eyes. Also, some anecdotally say that blue light glasses help reduce eye strain.

102.

Commit. Deliver. Repeat.

This is the simplest recipe for building trust. It applies to all work but it's downright critical for remote work. If you commit to doing something, you promise to do a quantifiable amount of work in a specific amount of time. When you deliver on that commitment, over and over, those around will trust you to do the same in the future.

103.

Share your calendar.

If you need to coordinate with your partner, spouse, or kids, shared calendars can keep you all on the same page. This is especially critical when you're inhabiting the same spaces. There are so many ways to share depending on the calendar you use. You can share all details, busy/free information, or share the calendars that make sense. Transparency can help you avoid miscommunication and add context to everyone's day.

104.

Be available to your team.

If you're a manager, be available to your team. In a distributed or hybrid workplace, this means making an extra effort to convey your availability. Keep your busy/free information updated in your calendar. When you're free, be responsive to requests for your time. This will help you generate a track record of availability. Schedule recurring 1:1 meetings with your direct reports, and hold them as planned. Similar guidance applies to team members. When you make yourself available and are responsive to your peers, you communicate that you're a team player. Others will know they can rely on you when they need your skills and counsel.

105.

Need a break?
Hide your video.

If video conference calls are a part of your day, you might get tired of staring at yourself or others. After all, it's not natural for us to gaze into each other's eyes when we're together in real life. When it gets to be too much, minimize the video window so you can still see what's shared (and others can still see you), or turn off your video if you want to see others but not yourself. You can still collaborate actively with your voice, and that's just fine.

106.

Send a daily text.

This tip was inspired by Tim Ferriss' interview with Hugh Jackman. Every morning, Hugh writes or types a summary of his day using the past tense as if it's already happened. After using this tip for the greater part of a year, I've come away with three benefits. First, by putting things out into the universe, using the past tense, you help to manifest them. Second, you can be more prepared for the day ahead by thinking about what it entails. And last, it helps keep you accountable, especially for the tough tasks you say you'll do.

107.

Listen at least as much as you talk.

Set a goal to listen to others in a conversation as much as, if not more than, you talk. You can learn so much more, and often arrive at a better conclusion, than if you dominated the conversation. After all, the interaction could have been asynchronous if only one of you is talking. Make sure that everyone has a voice, too. A simple prompt of "What do you think?" can bring a quieter person into center stage and give you more insight.

108.

Fuel wisely.

You may be more aware of your hunger when you're working without the distractions of an office. Avoid the temptation to graze throughout the day. Opt instead for planned healthy snacks if you need them between meals. Think in advance about what you plan to eat and you'll be less likely to reach for unhealthy options. If you have a certain food that's your kryptonite, leave it off your grocery list. You'll be better off if it's not hollering for you every day.

109.

Proclaim your OOO status.

Going to be out of the office (OOO) on vacation or handling an illness or emergency? Try your best to set your out-of-office status on email and collaboration platforms. Tell people how long you'll be out and who they can contact in the meantime if they have questions. If you're in a role that's difficult to back up, consider listing your personal contact information in case of emergency.

110.

Set expectations for deferred actions.

When you can't react immediately to a request, set expectations for when you can. Respond, "I'll get the answer for you" or "I can do this later for you" and provide a time frame. This type of caring response – instead of a curt "I don't know" or "I can't do that" – gives the requester an assurance that they'll get an answer or action later.

111.

Soak, then scrub.

Confronted with a stubborn baked-on, burned-in mess? It's far easier to soak a pot or pan instead of scrubbing for ages. Soak, then scrub. The business analogy: when faced with a difficult problem, compartmentalize it and leave it for a bit. Go for a walk or a run, or work on something different. It'll still be there when you come back and the answer may come to you in the meantime.

112.

Find the balance between inadequacy and perfection.

How do you know when you're done with a job? As with most things in life, it's an art form. Painting is a great analogy. Will one coat of paint cover the wall? Great. Stop at one coat. But, when the job requires two coats, never stop at one. If you notice, others will too. There's a balance between inadequacy and perfection. Find the balance between one and two coats of paint and you'll achieve consistency in your performance.

113.

Keep calm in a crisis.

Do you know those moments when time narrows and your blood pressure elevates? Crises can strike at any time, at work or at home. Little good comes from being the one who panics. Levelheadedness in the face of stress will help set the tone for others around you.

114.

You have to leave off before you can pick up.

There are times when your work will not logically conclude at the end of your workday. This can be tough if it's a particularly vexing problem. If you must leave something undone, take steps to be fully present for yourself and those around you during your non-working time. Unburden your mind by leaving notes to yourself about what your immediate next steps are when you pick up where you left off. Make a plan in your calendar to finish the work. Then, leave.

115.

Make lunch reservations for yourself.

You know that feeling: it's lunchtime. You look at your calendar and realize with dismay that you don't have enough time to take a break. Safeguard this time by making a recurring appointment for yourself in your calendar. Others may think twice before booking an appointment when you're busy, and you'll be grateful to be able to take the midday break you need.

116.

Know your audience.

Whether encountering a new country, culture, or person, know your audience. Don't go in cold. Do your research. Ask questions. It'll help tailor your interactions for success. No matter what you learn, it will likely be useful at some point down the road.

117.

Don't be bullied into traveling more often than necessary.

If you work in a hybrid workplace or are the outlier in a mostly onsite company, you're likely to travel. There is a fine line to trip frequency, though. Travel should benefit both parties. The desire for "face time" usually cuts one way, so balance travel with your need to be at home and productive. Seeing others in real life is great: teams work well when social connections are strong. It doesn't take much, just a few social interactions and working together in the same place for a few days. When you travel, make a point to meet people who joined the team recently.

118.

Trumpet your achievements.

When you're not in a physical space together, you can't have someone "pop by" and see what you're working on. Nobody can check out the whiteboard of notes in the conference room. That means you have to be far more intentional about sharing your team's achievements. You can send a simple targeted email at the end of a project or publish a periodic newsletter. Managing an internal website dedicated to project-level sharing can be rather effective, too. You can also host virtual events – roadshows, if you will – to share synchronously.

119.

Focus inward to be better outward.

Mindfulness, meditation, and mental exercises can help counter negativity in your life. See what works best for you. It can be difficult to non-judgmentally stay in the present, as mindfulness calls for. Practice makes better, though. It can help relax you, reduce anxiety, and center your mind.

120.

Grow and cultivate your network.

Networking is important. A solid network of social and professional connections can pay long-term dividends. Your network might help you blaze a career path. It might help you land a big deal. You might play a major role in helping someone else achieve their dreams. And someone you know professionally may be the one to throw you a lifeline when you need it the most.

121.

Get proper task lighting.

Depending on where you live and the time of year, you might start working as the sun comes up and quit after it gets dark. Think about the task lighting you'll need at your desk, no matter the light outside. Adjustability, aesthetics, color temperature, and illuminance are all factors. Read reviews to find an adequate solution for your situation.

122.

Create an onboarding guide.

Think about when you first joined your team. What applications did you need installed? What systems did you need an account on? What did you need a demo of? And what institutional knowledge was critical to you coming up to speed? When you onboard someone new, they're going to have the exact same questions. Create a collaborative space where this information can persist. New hires will find this space invaluable during onboarding. They can update it with anything they think others would appreciate, too.

123.

Size up your desk.

When selecting a desk, think about how much space you'll need for work. Will you need to have space for a larger monitor, external keyboard, and laptop? Where will lighting go? Will you always be doing computer-based work, or will you need space for reading, drawing, or writing on paper? These considerations will lead you to an ideal size. If you think you might enjoy standing at any time of the day, consider a motorized standing desk. You'll appreciate the flexibility even if you're only standing for a few hours a day. A mix of sitting and standing is best, after all. Lastly, think about material: glass, bamboo, wood, and composite all convey a certain feeling when you work at them.

124.

Design your way.

Home offices can have the polar opposite of a traditional office's design aesthetic. No off-white walls or tan cubicle dividers for you, right? Make your space yours: start with the walls. Paint them with colors you enjoy. Hang things that are meaningful and inspirational: posters, paintings, maps, photos, or designs. Put things you love on your bookshelves, and orient your favorite books with the cover facing out. You'll look at these wonderful things for hours each day, and some of them are bound to be conversation starters when you're on video calls.

125.

Use technology to compartmentalize personal and professional work.

It can be difficult to have a single computer: it's too easy to context switch between leisure and work tasks. If you have the luxury of dedicated hardware for personal and professional work, you're already ahead of the game. It's effective to put one to sleep, or out of sight, when you're supposed to be working on the other. If you have a single device, it may support multiple desktops or profiles. Set up your screens based on your task flow and you'll cut down on distractions.

126.

Reward yourself.

Multitasking is the mother of all distractions. Your attention flits from task to task, and all tasks can suffer as a result. Tame your tendency to multitask: get rid of distractions and commit to completing one task before switching to another. Better yet, promise yourself a reward when you're done. When you promise yourself something on completion, you'll be more likely to stay on track. A walk, a quick errand, or a much-needed refill of your coffee can be great ways to reward yourself.

127.

Declutter your workspace.

This is less a tip about messy desks versus clean desks and more of a general rule of thumb. If you see something in your periphery – something that reminds you that you have other things to do – you're not focused on your task. Hide the things that can pull your attention. Everything else? That's totally up to you.

128.

Can you hear me now?

You speak with others using a cell phone, computer, or a device that supports streaming audio. Regardless of the path your voice takes, make sure your voice quality is as good as possible. It's one of the impressions you make when you're working remotely. You don't want to be the person with the horrible voice connection. Think about quality (it varies with Bluetooth accessories and shock-mounted external mics) and portability. It's nice to be untethered from your desk, but not at the expense of voice quality. Finally, test your setup with someone you trust.

129.

Move data like a pro.

Remember the promise of a paperless office? We're almost there! Well, we've been saying that for years, right? Throughout your career, you'll come across the need to move data around. You'll need to go from analog to digital, or from one digital format to another. It's worth learning the ins and outs of file formats. Learn how to export a file to a PDF and how to take a screenshot of your entire screen or a region of your screen. Create a zip file or an archive of many files. You may need to digitally deliver something that must be physically signed. Take a high-quality scan of the signed physical paper(s) with your phone (try TurboScan). Or, use a stylus to mark up the digital version on a tablet and export it as a new version.

130.

Don't leave doubts as to your whereabouts.

Flexibility is one of the key benefits of working remotely. Transparency is also important. Have an appointment that'll take you out of communication for a while during business hours? Update your availability in your calendar so others know that you're out, or at least busy. Don't be a slave to the green "presence" icon, either. It's okay to take a break without announcing it, but you owe it to your coworkers and managers to communicate longer stretches of unavailability. Don't overshare when you're communicating your status. You don't need to announce the details of your medical appointment or who you're enjoying lunch with.

131.

Amp up your hardware.

It's time to buy a new computer. Think first about the physical size you need. Is portability a concern? If you ever want to move to another spot to work, it is. Get the size that'll work for you. Then, if your budget supports it, get a configuration that's better than what you think you need. It's hard (or impossible) to upgrade processor speed, RAM, or disk space, so consider these up-front incremental costs as an investment in the future.

132.

Avoid filler material.

Time is the most precious commodity you have. If you've exhausted the agenda of a meeting (you have one of those, right?) before the planned end time, end the meeting. There's no need to prompt further discussion, tap dance, or provide filler material until the clock runs out. Often, this will result in the meeting running over. Instead, send everyone back to whatever they were doing. They'll thank you for it.

133.

Be wary of Wi-Fi.

When you're working on the run, connect to Wi-Fi hotspots you know and trust. Open networks can be used by hackers, so be careful when choosing a network to join. Larger companies like Starbucks, Barnes & Noble, Panera, and McDonald's have free Wi-Fi locations nationwide. You can also check wififreespot.com or specialty apps that help you find Wi-Fi. When all else fails, see if your cell phone plan supports tethering. It can be a great way to get online in a pinch, but be careful with data usage if you lack an unlimited data plan.

134.

Speak well.

You'll have many opportunities to speak to others, virtually and in-person, during your career. If you're uncomfortable with public speaking (and let's face it, if you're not in front of a mirror by yourself, it's public speaking) take a course or two to get more comfortable. Speak more slowly and deliberately than you think you should. Enunciate. Vary your tone and cadence (no monotone delivery). Make eye contact. Move around if you can. But most importantly, have fun with it!

135.

Manage your email.

Don't let your email manage you. There are many approaches to email management. You know it's working when you don't have to apologize for not seeing something important, or not holding up something that you've been asked to weigh in on. There are many benefits to keeping conversations in collaboration platforms instead of email. Over time, the balance of your communication may shift from email to these more modern platforms. While you're in email-land, though, use rules, labels, notifications, and folders to your advantage.

136.

Randomness can be fun.

If you must have daily meetings, shift up the format to keep things fresh. Keep the meetings efficient and brief, of course, but try having your team share updates in a random order. With a predictable order, people tune out unless it's their turn to talk. Randomness keeps attendees alert and adds an element of unpredictability (and fun) to the proceedings.

137.

Keep your kudos.

Businesses publish testimonials, share success stories on social media, and post letters of praise on their walls. Your work should be no different. When you get positive feedback from your manager or colleague, or a thank you note from another group or a client, keep track of it. Forward messages of praise to your manager for visibility. Then, file them away in a "Kudos" folder for annual review time or anytime you need an emotional boost.

138.

Ask to be involved.

If you'd like to work on a new project, ask
how you can help. If you hear about a
meeting that you think you should be at, your
exclusion might be an oversight. Ask to be
included and then contribute to the
conversation once you're there. After you
have several of these interactions, you'll need
to be less proactive to have a seat at the table.

139.

Use social media to keep tabs on your industry.

Social doesn't have to be 100% social. Follow thought leaders in your field and find people who are doing work that you already do, or want to do. Read what they publish and you'll get a good sense of industry trends. You can also share your own material and establish a reputation.

140.

Support industry publications.

You might get printed editions of your favorite publications, but digital subscriptions can be easier. Sign up for the email lists of your favorite publishers. You might consider paying for a few digital subscriptions for publications that are really important to you. Several companies offer paid subscriptions for current and back editions. Check your local library, too. They may offer free digital magazine subscriptions as part of your membership.

141.

Leverage your benefits.

Your workplace may offer extra benefits on top of medical, dental, and time off. Look for discounts on cell phone plans, entertainment, travel, and more. Also, some companies will match your charitable contributions. These are all wonderful ways to maximize your compensation.

142.

Pursue personal projects.

Do you want to learn a new language, skill, or have an idea for a project? Just get started. Take the initiative to make progress during nights and weekends. Use the time to learn something new and put it into practice on your own schedule. It'll show your current or potential employers that you're a lifelong learner.

143.

Set a goal to meet someone new.

Set a goal to meet someone new every so often. It might be weekly, monthly ... whatever frequency you're comfortable with. Then, do something social with them! The person you meet would ideally be new, but you can also rekindle a past business or personal relationship. This is a great way to expand your network and keep it healthy.

144.

Take care of your mental health.

What does your health insurance policy cover for mental and behavioral health? As a manager, this is good information to know and share with your team. Be transparent about the availability of these services and you'll help erase the stigma associated with them. As an employee, if you're struggling with mental health, do this legwork yourself and see what's available to you. Even if you have to use your own funds, your mental health is as important, if not more so, than your physical health. Reach out when you need help and take care of yourself.

145.

Overcome distance bias.

Distance bias is the tendency to favor people who are closer to us in time and space. As a remote worker, you'll experience this at some point in your career. Counter it by being vocal. Use one-on-one time with your manager to share recent accomplishments, development goals, and future plans. Get involved in any way you can. As a manager, you can help your remote employees transcend distance bias. Cede the spotlight to them in presentations, demos, and other public forums. Be inclusive of their opinions when making decisions in a hybrid setting.

146.

Know the time around the world.

It's a big world and chances are you'll find yourself working with someone in a different time zone. Scheduling meetings is another topic, but simply being aware of the time where your colleague works is a great way to deepen connection. Use the proper salutation for the time of day (good morning vs. good afternoon) and know when someone's working earlier or later than they usually do. It's a great conversation starter if it's close to quitting time for your colleague, or close to lunch time. There are so many desktop, mobile, and wrist-based solutions for calculating times across time zones. Pick one and enjoy knowing what time it is at a glance.

147.

Keep a clean office.

In a traditional office, someone else likely does the cleaning. Every day, someone vacuums, dusts, collects trash, waters plants, and keeps the fridge clear of aspirational science experiments. Nobody is going to do that for you when you're on your own at home. If you're the exception to this rule, congratulations! So, make a schedule that works for you. Spend a couple minutes every few weeks and you'll maintain a beautiful, dust-free, plant-rich, trash-free space.

148.

Manifest your promotion.

Have you heard of the concept of manifesting? Or know the value of creating and conspicuously posting a vision board? Find out what your next level of promotion at work entails and post it where you will see it every day. By keeping your goals front and center, you'll help breathe life into them.

149.

Have fun.

We're not all comedians, but a little appropriate humor goes a long way. We're all human. When we're too serious about our jobs and remove the humanity from the equation, it feels like work. When we can have fun while we're working, we establish more rapport with others and it feels a whole lot better. Have fun with each other!

150.

Set clear expectations in a persistent place.

You need to set clear expectations as a manager of a distributed team. What are the results you'll measure your team by? When your team knows what the desired results are – the target, if you will – they'll be more likely to deliver. It's hard to hit a target you cannot see.

151.

Use collaboration features to get participants participating.

Your collaboration software may have features that can help engage participants. Not everyone likes to talk all the time, of course. Use voting (digital or analog), hand-raising features, whiteboards, and breakout rooms. They all can help keep everyone more involved in the conversation.

152.

Recognize imposter syndrome for what it is.

Do you doubt your abilities? Does it feel difficult to accept your accomplishments as evidence of your competence? These feelings can come to the fore when you're not physically with others, though they can afflict anyone. Start by not judging yourself for having these feelings. Treat yourself with kindness and compassion. Try to examine what underlies the feelings. They may show you things you should change. You might need to reframe your mindset, recognizing you've worked hard and deserve what you have. You might see it as a catalyst to look for the next step in your career, find better ways to deal with stress, or share with someone you trust. If it persists, find a therapist who can help you deal with those thoughts and feelings.

153.

Invest in collaboration technology.

Be a technology leader when it comes to helping your people connect. Tools come and go, but there will always be technology that helps us connect in real time or asynchronously. Think about what your team needs. Video, screen sharing, document storage, and breakout rooms are all becoming table stakes. Invest in the technology to address those needs. Your team will feel a closer connection to each other and to the material they need to do their jobs.

154.

Safeguard your flow time.

There are certain times of day that are best for your productivity, right? Certain conditions under which you thrive? Create those conditions and safeguard them. You might work best in the morning or afternoon, and probably enjoy large swaths of uninterrupted time. Block that time in your calendar and don't let it go.

155.

Don't do personal work on business networks.

Relegate your shopping, searching, and social networking to your personal devices. It can be tempting to use your work computer to look up a great dinner place, check personal email, shop Cyber Monday, or mindlessly scroll through social media on your lunch break. Don't do it, though. Your business's network is for business. Your employer could be watching you conduct personal work, opening you to scrutiny. You're also exposing the business network to potential security vulnerabilities.

156.

Remember the two magical words that can help clear up an offense.

Did you inadvertently offend someone? Perhaps it was in the heat of the moment in a tense discussion, or a communication misunderstanding, or a gaffe where you thought you were on mute. Whatever it is, get in front of it. It might be awkward to apologize and have an open discussion, but it sure beats letting it fester. Explain yourself, help others understand the situation, and move on. Luckily, there are two magic words that can help you start any conversation like this: "I'm sorry."

157.

Be the one who's willing to catch the ball.

A lot of success, whether virtual or in-person, comes from being the person who takes the lead. To use a baseball analogy, it's how you react to a pop fly to deep center field. You can be the one who yells, "Got it!" and positions themselves for the catch, or you can be the one who looks around first to see if anyone else is going to react. By being the one who's willing to catch the ball, you communicate you're a go-getter. You have initiative. You have ideas. And you'll get invited to play the game far more often.

158.

Evolve.

Nothing hurts an organization's health more than saying, "Well, that's how we've always done it." Time marches on. So do the options for managing yourself, your work, your team, and your business. Evolve to keep on top of your game. Evaluate periodically. Keep what works. Ditch what doesn't.

159.

Mark milestones.

Life is sweeter when you celebrate special occasions as a group. Take note of birthdays, milestone work anniversaries, and major life events like an engagement, marriage, or a new child. These are all wonderful reasons to gather virtually and fête your colleagues. For major events, you might take up a collection among team members and present the honoree with a gift card. You can also send around an allowance for your team to get a cup of coffee, slice of cake, or some lunch to share as a group as you celebrate.

160.

Keep your software up to date.

Software updates are important. They protect your computer and your phone from security vulnerabilities, resolve bugs, and provide new enhancements that can help your productivity. To mitigate the stress of an update, especially a major one, perform a backup of your computer or phone before you start. Don't install updates as soon as they're available: wait a few days. This gives the provider a chance to remedy any upgrade problems.

161.

Don't let personal projects derail your workday.

You might love cooking elaborate meals, doing complex landscaping, or be in the midst of a massive home improvement project. Don't let these types of extracurricular activities derail your work day. If you have to spend significant time on these, that's what time off is for. That doesn't mean you can't progress on them and work the same day, though. You lack a commute, so you can spend pre-work time getting something done. Lunch can be prime time for tackling something that takes under an hour. Be wary of starting something you can't finish before you're expected to be at work and productive.

162.

Create systems to prevent intrusion.

You're about to summarize the key point in a very important meeting when disaster strikes. Your spouse, roommate, child, or pet (or any combination, frankly) bursts into the room! They interrupt your flow and call attendees' attention away from you. This happens every day, but it doesn't have to. Communicate your "do not disturb" status with those around you. Use a shared calendar, a conversation, or a sign or indicator on the closed (and locked, if possible) door.

163.

Be wary of burnout.

According to the World Health Organization, burnout is "a syndrome conceptualized as resulting from chronic workplace stress that has not been successfully managed." Watch for signs of burnout in yourself or on your team. Feel exhausted or depleted? Disconnected from your work? Cynical? Not performing well? Do not ignore these signs if you see them. Gallup cites five key causes, and they all have prescriptions for resolution: unfair treatment, unmanageable workload, unclear top-down communication, lack of manager support, and unreasonable deadlines and pressure.

164.

Use breaks to calm your mind.

Stepping away for a few moments during your workday? Use the time to do something that takes your mind off work-related things. Think about activities that relax you. Take a short walk in your garden or down your street. Sit in a shady spot on a hot day. Sketch or write in a notebook, or crack open a book you're eager to read. The goal is relaxation, leaving you fresh and ready for the rest of your day.

165.

Set deadlines.

Deadlines can be a great discipline creator. When you know when something is due, you're more likely to create the space to get it done. No deadline given? Give yourself one. There's nothing worse than getting a request to do something "whenever you get a chance." Make that chance a surety by doing it right then, or adding a date-driven task or calendar appointment to remind you.

166.

Hit the hay (and rise and shine) every day at consistent times.

Try not to mess with your schedule depending on the day of the week. If you go to bed at a consistent time each night, your brain will learn what to expect. We humans thrive on routine! Same goes for getting up. Set an alarm whether it's a work day or not, and every day will feel just right.

167.

Warm up your emails.

When you write emails, you might inadvertently use a less friendly style than you intended. Go back and look at your correspondence. Is it coming off the way you'd hoped? Written words don't have the tone and texture that spoken words do. You have to be intentional about warming up your emails. For suggestions, search for "warm tone in emails".

168.

Quantify the value of distributed work.

Metrics matter. Do you know the value of distributed work from your perspective as a worker? How about as an employer? It takes just a few minutes with a spreadsheet to calculate the savings on commuting, clothing, and meals out. If you want a more comprehensive calculation, head over to the Workplace Savings Calculator*.

globalworkplaceanalytics.com/roi

169.

Ensure stability in your audio connection.

We can all do without video if needed, but if audio fails it's a big problem. If you'll be talking a lot in a meeting, ensure that you're using the most stable audio connection possible. If you're in a place with great bandwidth, use the streaming options on your device. Otherwise, connect on a landline or with your cell phone so you'll be less likely to experience audio issues. Also, have a plan to switch your connection if your primary way of connecting fails.

170.

Find the magic in unstructured time.

When all your time is planned for you (or by you), you can miss out on time to think freely. When did inspiration strike you last? Chances are, it wasn't during a hectic day of meetings. Allocate unstructured time for you to focus on your own work. It may simply be time to think, but you'll create the space for novel ideas to form, emerge, and mature.

171.

Give the gift of focused, unbounded attention.

Think about the last time you met with someone, be they a spouse, friend, colleague, medical professional, or a service worker. Were they patient and attentive, or impatient and distracted? Did it seem like they had all the time in the world for you, or did the interaction seem rushed? When you experience the former, you feel like it's a high-quality interaction. You trust them. When you're with someone else, give them the gift of your attention. Clear the mental decks, so to speak, and focus on the interaction.

172.

Communicate directly with your clients and customers.

Who are your clients or customers? Whatever you call them, they're the people who'd miss you most if you ceased to do the work you do. Like the age-old saying "straight from the horse's mouth", it's best to get insights and feedback from a source as close as possible to them, if not directly. Then can you truly understand if the work you're doing aligns with their needs, or helps solve problems they may not know they have.

173.

Don't go in cold for tough discussions.

Not all business decisions or discussions can be had in the moment. If you have a difficult topic to cover as a group, talk to individuals in advance to get their thoughts. This is an equity play, too: you'll get input from the quieter and more reserved people on your team. Then, you can approach the topic with a more well-rounded understanding of the broad themes at play. Still not sure? Bounce your ideas off a mentor or someone else whose judgment you trust.

174.

Default to sharing in async tools.

You have a great collaboration platform, right? If you use it mostly as an email replacement, for direct person-to-person communication, you're missing out. Try bringing conversations out into the open, where people can pop in and out of a group as needed. It's a great transparency move, and nobody will feel as if they're being left out of the loop. If you do need to meet one-on-one or synchronously as a group, remember to go back and share the results in the collaboration thread.

175.

Plan trips.

Planning a trip can work wonders for your mental health. When you take the time to plan a purposeful trip, it gives your mind something to look forward to. Think about when you traveled last. Did it give you an enhanced appreciation for what you have? Or did it spur you to do something to improve your current home? Travel can offer perspective, creativity, and clarity, especially travel to a new location.

176.

Remote work isn't the problem.

Something not working as well as it could? Don't default to blaming remote work. There's likely an underlying issue that's causing the symptoms you're seeing. Look at your communication, management style, process, culture, and the way your team makes decisions. Being face-to-face may alleviate some communication issues, but it'll never get to the root of a more systemic problem.

177.

Work with people who are smarter, faster, and better than you.

When you work alongside more experienced people (enter smarter, faster, and better), you, in turn, become smarter, faster, and better. Don't be afraid to aspire to their skill or experience level. They did it, and with time, effort, and patience, you can too.

178.

Validate your team.

Recall a time when you received praise for doing a good job. Felt good, right? When you recognize and validate what your team has done, you boost their esteem, increase job satisfaction, and motivate them to repeat the feat. It has the opposite effect when you don't recognize these efforts with sincere thanks. Validation doesn't have to cost much, or anything, for that matter. Words are free. A simple expression of "Wow, you took on a tough task and hit it out of the park" can do quite nicely. You can also use concierge coupons, virtual pizza parties, or small gifts to recognize significant achievements.

179.

When in doubt, share.

If you think your manager or peer might want to know something (emphasis on might), take the opportunity to communicate it to them. Trust your gut on communicating status, priorities, and deadlines. The added transparency contributes to an inclusive environment. Bonus points if you share in a public async forum so everyone can see what you've shared.

180.

Don't give your employer a reason to surveil you.

As an employee, you should want to do your very best work every day, regardless of where you're sitting vis-à-vis your peers. However, if you think that working remotely means you can slack off more than your office-bound counterparts, working remotely is not for you. Some employer distrust comes from a history of dealing with workers who want to get away with doing less than their peers. That has employers asking, "How can I trust that you're working if I can't actually see you working?" So work, and trust will follow.

181.

Use a timer to get focused work done.

Timers can be a very effective tool to help you do focused work. Put your phone in airplane mode (or just leave it behind), close all the apps you're not using, and don't stop working on the task until the time is up.

182.

Embrace the midday power nap.

You might experience a lull in your energy levels in the early afternoon. A short power nap – limited to 15-30 minutes to avoid going into a deep sleep – can save your afternoon. Unfortunately, there's a stigma in some circles around midday napping. These siestas help reduce stress, improve cognition, and can position you to have a more efficient afternoon. It beats suffering through work when you're tired and prone to slack off doing non-work activities. So set a timer, find a quiet spot, and get a few minutes of midday shut-eye.

183.

Change your environment to boost productivity.

Small changes can make big differences in your productivity. Try changing your lighting, music, or ambient noise (or lack of noise) around you. Reorganize your desk, or shift from sitting to standing. These small adjustments may boost your productivity when you need it most.

184.

Look for the filling in praise sandwiches.

It's evaluation time. You may evaluate your own performance if you're solo, or get feedback from your manager or peers. Ask for specific ways in which you can improve. Feedback may come to you as a praise sandwich, where negative feedback is hidden amidst positive feedback. Minimize the bread of that sandwich and focus on the filling. That's where the true, actionable feedback lives.

185.

Embrace location independence.

Working remotely doesn't mean you have to sit in a chair alone in your home office, day after day. Take advantage of opportunities to relocate. Go to another room, library, coffee shop, coworking space, a shaded table outside your door, or a quiet park bench. You can do great work anywhere, and sometimes you can get the boost you need by changing your scenery. Plus, you may get a little socialization in the process, which is always a good thing.

186.

Cancel the noise.

There'll be times when you can't tune out the world when you need to. You might be home and the neighbor fires up their leaf blower. Or at the coffee shop and the people nearby are a little too loud. Or trying to be productive while you're on a bus, train, or plane. When noise intrudes, noise-canceling headphones can come to the rescue. Read reviews carefully and think about what you'd be most comfortable with, either an over-the-ear or in-ear pair.

187.

Get a nice vessel for your drinks.

You'll use the same mug or glass every day for water, tea, or coffee. Treat yourself to a vessel you'll appreciate daily. Get something with a personal touch, a bit of technology (self-warming mugs are awesome), or a nice double-wall to keep cold drinks from sweating all over your fine desktop.

188.

Share your screen like a pro.

When you're sharing your screen with others, use a few tips to help things go more smoothly. Share only the application you want to so you don't inadvertently share something you didn't intend. If you must share your entire screen, quit applications like chat or email that could pop up notifications and interrupt your flow. Lastly, be aware of screen resolution. If you have a huge external monitor, sharing a window from there might not give your guests a close-up view. Instead, try sharing the window from your laptop's screen, which likely has a better resolution for sharing.

189.

Practice good digital security.

It's so important to know what good digital security looks like. So many bad actors try to get into your computer and network. They use email attachments, phishing links in the body of emails, and social engineering via email, text, or voice. Don't fall for it. Before you click on a link or attachment from someone you don't know, check with someone who can tell you for sure. If there's even a shred of doubt, delete it.

190.

Use note-taking apps.

Like a good task manager, a good note-taking app will let you sync across devices, embed images and rich text, add links to text, and search. Gone are the days of using sticky notes and placing them all over your desktop. You might enjoy the tactile feel of a real notebook, too, but will sacrifice the ability to search and backup your carefully-taken notes.

191.

Demonstrate self-sufficiency.

Self-sufficiency is one of the hallmark traits that can help you land – and keep – a remote job. Look for instances in your personal and professional life where you've taken the lead on getting something done. On schedule, as specified, within budget ... all that good stuff. Document your successes so you can recall how you took ownership and accomplished your task without a ton of external motivation. Look for opportunities in your work to be proactive and take the lead on delivering value.

192.

Refactor.

Refactoring, in the world of software development, is the process of improving the structure, legibility, elegance, or maintainability of your code without affecting what it does. In other words, improving the mechanics, not the message. Refactoring can apply to many domains, including emails, requirements, presentations, and designs. Take time to do your best work, and then ask yourself: is there a way I can improve this? Refactoring takes time but can be worth it in the long run.

193.

We, not I.

Unless you're on your own as an entrepreneur, work is not a solo effort. You're likely part of a team, and when you present your team's work to others, represent the work as a team effort. Use "we" to describe what you've done, not "I". We did this, we did that, and next, we plan on doing another awesome thing.

194.

Try asynchronous status updates.

It's tempting to get everyone together at the same time every day to "go around the room" and give a daily status. However, it can be an immense drain on everyone's time, and over time, participants may view it as unproductive. They may tune out after sharing their update. Instead, try asynchronous updates, where everyone shares a quick bullet summary in a collaboration platform, at the beginning of their day, of what they're working on. Everyone else can catch up at their leisure. These types of updates can be searched, tag projects, link to web pages where needed, and mention people. If you've been out on vacation, they allow you to catch up on what you missed. Use your meeting time, if needed, for follow-ups that require real-time collaboration.

195.

Recognize your biases.

We all have biases. They're part of our natural circuitry and are typically unconscious stereotypes. In a professional environment, the key is to recognize them and take steps to avoid or mitigate them. Ageism, sexism, and racism are all rooted in unconscious bias and are toxic to a safe, effective workplace. Other biases abound, too. Look for professional development opportunities to be able to recognize and address bias in your workplace.

196.

Avoid groupthink when making decisions.

Be aware of the effects of groupthink when you hope to build a true consensus in a meeting. It can be hard for some people to speak up in a group setting for fear of being perceived differently. Some may hesitate to raise an unpopular opinion or an "out of the box" idea. These can be amplified when strong personalities are present. The group may tend to adopt the viewpoint of stronger personalities. Haven't heard from a participant and suspect this dynamic? Ask for their opinion in the meeting, or solicit their feedback in advance. Cultivate a psychologically safe space where you can discuss diverse viewpoints without fear.

197.

Treat yourself to a work-oriented "go bag".

How do you pack up your things when you head to a coffee shop, a library, company headquarters, or a client office? Get a nice "go bag" that's professional and smart. It should comfortably fit everything you need for your time away from your home office. Think about toting your laptop, devices, mouse, charge cables, wallet, and other creature comforts.

198.

Don't cram for your professional development.

You set a goal for the year to learn some new things, right? Fast-forward to November and you may find you've been "all work and no learn" and can't show any progress. Create a professional development schedule for yourself. Set aside recurring time on your calendar to keep yourself accountable. This simple act should help you stay on track and make incremental progress.

199.

Be responsible with company money.

At some point in your career, you'll need to spend company money on purchases, travel, or events. Be a good steward of those monetary resources and spend them as if they were your own. If there's a doubt in your mind if an expenditure is okay, it's probably not. Also related to company money: become familiar with what expenses qualify for reimbursement. You might find that some home office expenses are reimbursable.

200.

Give kudos.

An earlier tip covered the importance of keeping your kudos. If nobody gave them, though, there'd be none to keep. When your colleagues, partners, or clients really shine, take a moment to recognize their efforts. Send them a direct note and copy their manager to let them know just how much of a difference they made. This can extend into non-work activities, too. Reviews make the world go 'round, and if someone has gone above and beyond, give them a boost with a solid review.

201.

Give yourself time to catch up after taking time off.

Coming back from time off can be difficult. You might have the internal expectation that you should hit the ground running and be 100% productive from the moment you step in the virtual door. Remind yourself that you have to reduce your capacity and take time to catch up. You'll need to get through emails, understand decisions made in your absence, and reconnect with your colleagues. Your time away was well spent, and the time you spend reacclimatizing to work is exactly the same.

202.

Family comes first.

Work never comes before family. It's wonderful to spend more time with your spouse, significant other, children, and extended family as a simple byproduct of working remotely. That said, important events, emergencies, and mini-crises will make this perk all the more critical. Take time to fully disengage from work and be with your family, especially when it matters the most. Work can wait.

203.

Decline appointments when you'll be out.

It's no fun to get to a meeting and realize that key participants are not there because they failed to notify the meeting organizer. When you'll be out for vacation, holiday, a personal day, or sick time, add an all-day appointment to your calendar and mark your status as out of office. Decline any appointments where others will miss you.

204.

Don't tolerate insults, harassment, or bullying.

Have you been exposed to insults, harassment, or bullying at work? Have you been a witness to this behavior, or had someone who worked for you report it? Don't keep it to yourself. Documentation is your friend. Carefully and objectively document the behavior you've seen and keep everything in a secure place. If the incident is a one-off you can try to sort it out person-to-person. If it's a pattern, though, it's time to get HR involved.

205.

Overcommunicate.

When you communicate asynchronously – in email, chat, or in a collaborative document – the recipients don't have the luxury of real-time interaction with you to clear up ambiguity. Think about the information you used to come to your conclusions and add those to the documentation. Links, screenshots, and other annotations can be critical to comprehension. When you think you're sharing more than what's necessary, you're probably sharing the correct amount.

206.

Use project management software.

Chances are, you take on projects as part of your business. Project management software can help you keep track of your short- and long-term aspirations. They can be useful for anyone from solo practitioners to larger companies. When you break down your projects into manageable chunks and have proper software in place, you can effectively delegate, assign, discuss, document, and track progress.

207.

Amp up your avatar.

Avatars are everywhere, from social media, to address books, to project management systems. They're a part of your personal brand. If you leave yours as the default – an illustration of a person, your initials, or an abstract image – you're selling your brand short. Use a recognizable, professional photo of yourself. When everyone on a team does this, it's far easier to recognize them online and in person.

208.

Switch up your tasks, projects, and surroundings.

When you work on the same thing day in and day out, your days can feel quite the same. What used to be challenging and extraordinary can turn into the ordinary. The inherent variety of working on diverse tasks and projects with different people can help jumpstart things. If you find yourself in a rut, look around for opportunities to inject some newness into your workday.

209.

Know your clients.

You work with people all day long. They're your clients! Depending on your role, they may be internal, external, stakeholders, or paid subscribers to your product or service. Get to know them and keep things straight by using a customer relationship management (CRM) solution. You might need an enterprise-class solution for an international sales team. You might be on your own and keep these details in a spreadsheet. Regardless, keep your system tidy, updated, and tailored for your use.

210.

Designate a notetaker.

When you're leading a collaboration session, designate a notetaker, if not yourself. They should capture the discussion as it evolves and record decisions. When everyone can review notes captured in real-time, it adds a cool interactive dimension and reduces the risk of misunderstandings.

211.

Look into the lens.

When you're leading or participating in a hybrid meeting, don't forget those who are participating on camera. When you focus your gaze only on the others in the room with you, it can make video participants feel excluded. Look to the camera periodically to address them directly, just as you would scan the entire room if you were giving a presentation.

212.

Use a VPN when safety is paramount.

Public Wi-Fi can be a boon for hackers. If you don't already use a VPN, get one for when you're working on public Wi-Fi, or working on material that's internal use only from your home network. When a VPN is on, anyone who's on the same network can't see what you're up to. Data is encrypted while you're connected, and is therefore unreadable.

213.

Ask for feedback.

Are you not getting feedback, or getting feedback that's not actionable? Ask for it as close as possible to the event that you'd like feedback about. Perhaps you've delivered a presentation, led a meeting, or finished a big project. Ask others how it went, and what things you could improve upon that would make it go even better. When you ask for this information, you also send a signal that you care about improving. That's a good thing for promotion and career development.

214.

If you need something to be your most productive, ask.

Is there something that would improve your ability to get your job done? Ask for it. Some companies offer a budget for this kind of thing, but others don't. Whether it's hardware-related (computer, keyboard, monitor, or another accessory) or related to working in your space (desk, anti-fatigue mat, or another ergonomic improvement), you won't get it if you don't bring it up. If all else fails, budget for it and make some purchases on your own. You won't regret anything that improves your work.

215.

Know when to use
cc: and bcc: fields.

If you must use email, keep the recipient list tight. Only cc (carbon copy) those who need to be aware of what's being communicated, but not directly participate in the discourse. Deescalate, or make the recipient list shorter, when you need to narrow the conversation. Escalation occurs when, in the course of a thread, you add someone because you realize they should be aware. If doing this as a reply all, add their name to the top of the email so others know they've been added, and why. It may be better, though, to forward them the thread along with a note so they can get caught up without having to read the whole thing. Bcc should only be used for newsletters or other cases where you don't expect a response, never to quietly add someone to the communication. If someone who's been bcc'd replies all, the jig is up.

216.

Inspire your team.

Make a space where your team can share with each other. As we all learned in kindergarten, "sharing is caring." It's important to share things outside of your core work deliverables so it's not just another status meeting. Share something you heard or saw, something you created outside of work, or something you learned that'll help others in the pursuit of their goals. Aim to have your sharing be inspirational, novel, and unique.

217.

Check in on your team's welfare.

Team leaders should drop in on their team members at regular intervals to simply check-in. It could be done as part of a one-on-one, but also could be casually scheduled, just as if you'd bumped into each other in the office. The purpose is not to check in on work, but rather, life. How are they doing emotionally? What non-work activities are they into? What stressors are at play for them? You, in turn, can share your own thoughts on these topics. By caring for the whole person, you show respect for them and help enhance trust in your relationship.

218.

Eat your own dog food.

It's important to "walk a mile" in your customer's shoes. Whether it's a website, application, a call center, or an in-person process, go through the process as your customers do. Only then will you understand what works, what doesn't, and have the context to understand consumer feedback.

219.

Use a password manager.

There's nothing worse for security than using the same password for many websites and applications. Instead, turn to a password manager. They'll help you use more secure passwords and have them auto-fill when you're prompted. Password managers typically sync between your devices and computers, too, so you can always have passwords when you need them. Choose a secure master password you won't forget. For an extra layer of security (for example, banking), turn on two-factor authentication.

220.

Plan your day the night before.

If you're a master at dividing work and play, you already know you shouldn't be looking at work-related applications during your downtime. However, glance at the day ahead and get a sense of your schedule. You might need to coordinate personal appointments, negotiate the use of a car, or shuffle some things around.

221.

Check out Massive Open Online Courses (MOOCs)

Think you're done with classes because you graduated from primary school or college? Maybe. But maybe not. Many colleges and universities offer free online courses that might be interesting. They can be great for your ongoing professional development. Find courses on Coursera, edX, and FutureLearn. A quick search for "free online college courses" will unearth online curriculum from esteemed universities and companies.

222.

Tip well.

The physical connections you have to your local community are important. When you interact with others, especially in the service industry, provide customary tips for a job well done (or more, for a job extraordinarily well done). Service workers work hard, and anyone who's worked in an industry that relies on tips knows the particular value of that currency. This is especially important in the context of a coffee shop where you might work periodically. The baristas will remember your respectful demeanor and treat you accordingly.

223.

Get that temperature just right.

Controlling the temperature of your room is one of the biggest benefits of being remote. When you're in a space that's not your own, you don't have much control. In your own environment, you can adjust the thermostat when it's too cold or too warm. You can choose whether you have your shoes on or off. And you can decide whether the window is wide open, tightly shut, or open just enough to let in a soft breeze. Aah.

224.

Be accountable.

Don't throw your team under the bus. The buck stops with you. I've seen plenty of managers face down criticism of something their team did with classic deflection. There's always an excuse – a mitigating circumstance – but in your managerial role, you cannot go further than yourself. When reflecting on something that didn't go quite right, think about what role you played. Sure, the actual blunder was caused by one of your team or an external factor. But what could you have done differently to result in a different outcome? Chances are you can identify several things that you influenced (or could have influenced) and can learn from them.

225.

Be aware of inclusion for hybrid team meetings.

When you combine a conference room with remote participants, it can create a dichotomy of 'people in the room' vs. 'people at home.' If everyone participates virtually, there's no such dichotomy. Participants will feel a better sense of equality and inclusion. Be aware of this as you run meetings with disparate groups of onsite and remote participants. Do your best to include remote participants as readily as in-room participants.

226.

Ditch the anchor at your desk.

Are you a passive participant in a meeting? Will your face not be missed? Try ditching the anchor at your desk and do something else while you listen in. You can still get something else done while you focus on what's communicated. Light chores, outdoor walks, or light indoor fitness (elliptical, bike, rowing) are all fair game.

227.

Ruthlessly unsubscribe.

Emails and chat notifications inject so much noise into your day. Ruthlessly protect yourself by unsubscribing from emails you never read, and muting or leaving group chats that you don't need to be a part of. Don't worry: you'll get invited back if you're missed. Less noise is a good thing.

228.

Take time to introduce new team members.

When your team grows, let new teammates introduce themselves during all-hands meetings. It's a great way to welcome them to the team and get to know them a bit better. Share meaningful pictures, some personal and professional background, and favorite non-work activities. Don't forget about your existing team members, either. By giving them a periodic spotlight in these gatherings, you help the team to gel even better.

229.

Join a group outside of work.

Joining groups outside of work can help fulfill social and emotional needs. You'll find groups centered around religion, hobbies, or sports. Try community-oriented volunteer options like your local school, library, food pantry, Habitat for Humanity chapter, and fire department. As a side benefit, these activities can feed back into your professional life. People you meet in non-professional circles might need the professional services you offer. They can also be a source of referrals to someone they know who can use your skills.

230.

Create your own community.

What if you can't find a pre-established group that resonates with you? Create your own. You can use almost any activity as an avenue to creating community. All you need is "the thing" and at least one person to show up. If you've already identified a group of people, propose a recurring time to do an activity you love. Try coffee, breakfast or lunch groups; biking, running, or hiking groups; touristy things in your area like museums, points of interest, boat rides, wine tastings; game nights with spouses and significant others; group fitness, yoga, or pick-up basketball. Advertise it and start meeting. Share it on social, at a meetup, or on a bulletin board. It may take some time to get traction, but don't give up!

231.

Take the time to start a conversation.

Community doesn't happen by accident. Sometimes, you have to take the first step in starting a conversation. A smile in a coffee shop. Saying hello in the grocery store. A break to talk to someone working near you at a coworking space. Simply talking to someone can unearth common interests.

232.

Get vulnerable with friends.

When you meet with a friend, try to get beyond superficial conversation topics. Candid conversation cultivates closeness. Talking about your feelings, hopes, and fears can counter loneliness. You'll likely find that your friend, in turn, will be more open with you, too.

233.

Get those well visits in.

Your insurance likely covers well visits to your primary doctor, dentist, and eye doctor. Plus, you don't need to take a full day to get those things taken care of when you're not commuting to an office. Take advantage of those benefits and stay healthy!

234.

Eat well for optimal health.

You can go all-in and include probiotics and antioxidant-rich foods in your diet. Or you can opt to "eat a rainbow" and focus on whole foods. If it comes in a bag or a box, or if the ingredients list has more unpronounceable things than not, it's not as good for you as something from the produce aisle. Depending on where you live, a CSA (Community Supported Agriculture) may be an option for fresh produce. No matter your culinary preferences, remember that variety is good. Moderation is even better.

235.

Get rid of visual reminders that you have other things to do.

When you're working, clear your space of visual reminders of the non-work things you need to do. Those reminders can pull your focus when you're supposed to be doubling down on work. Personal calendars, to-do lists, and piles of laundry should all be tucked away for another time.

236.

Put a check and balance on device addiction.

Do you have an unhealthy relationship with your device(s)? You're not alone, and digital addiction is real. When you're scrolling through social media, you're not working. Turning off your notifications can go a long way toward cutting down on your usage. Is an app particularly time-draining for you? Uninstall it.

237.

Optimize your workspace's soundscape.

Is the silence deafening where you work? Put on some good music or something soothing to help get you into flow. You have total control over what you hear – or don't hear – while you're working. Sometimes you might want to crank up the loudest, bass-filled rock anthem you can find. Other times might call for the purest silence or some ambient noise. You can have it both ways, so experiment with what works and have fun with it.

238.

Organize your thoughts when writing something complex.

When writing something important, optimize the structure of what you're communicating. Did it take you a while to arrive at your conclusion? Think about all the data and logic that helped you get there. Structure your writing with the goal of similarly influencing the reader. You can tell when something has been organized this way. It doesn't meander. It is well thought out. It carves a neat path from the beginning to the end.

239.

Switch mediums when misunderstandings arise.

Know when to take things out of a medium where communication is no longer effective. Phone calls or video chat can help clear up misunderstandings far faster than asynchronous communication.

240.

Try to be unambiguous when you communicate.

You can head off potential communication issues by trying to be proactive and identify them before they arise. If you can interpret something in more than one way, it's likely that it will be. Read and re-read things when you write them. Make them as clear and concise as possible. If you're addressing someone for whom English is not a primary language, use words that are clear and common. Nobody should need to use a dictionary to find out what you mean.

241.

Question to the void.

Seek clarification if you read or hear
something and your inner voice says, "Yeah, I
still don't understand." Ask questions until
you can't ask questions anymore. Only then
will you have gotten to the point where things
are clearly understood.

242.

Use auto-reply when you'll be away.

Turn on your email auto-reply feature when you're going to be away. It may be a day, a week, or more, but it's a great way to let people know that you're gone. Include information about how they can get in touch with you or your designated backup (if that's important). For critical communications that you can't follow up on immediately, let people know you received it. Give them an estimate of when you will respond.

243.

Model the behavior you hope to see.

When you're in charge of a team, your team members look to you for signals of expected behavior. Sending emails at all hours of the day? You're sending a signal that you want to see the same from your team. Supporting a hybrid workplace, yet you're always in the office? You're sending a signal that remote work is not okay. It doesn't matter what you say, or how often you say it. It's what you do that matters most.

244.

Ask and answer: what do you want to do?

This is a fantastic icebreaker question to start talking about your career trajectory. Do you know the answer? If so, you can take proactive steps to get there. If you're happy where you are, that's good information, too. You can continue to grow and mature in your role, which is good for you and your team.

245.

Keep your meetings on schedule.

Are your meetings chronically running over their allotted time? If you ask if people can "go over" you're not likely to get honest answers. They might be technically able to stretch into overtime, but will they be happy about it? Probably not. Some may also defer to the most senior people on the call, too. Respect people's time and keep your meetings within their allocated slot. Tighten the agenda, don't let others derail the conversation, and start on time.

246.

Confront management by fear.

Is fear entrenched as a quality of your workplace culture? It's a toxic ingredient and causes burnout, mental instability, unhappiness, and a lack of motivation. Sure, in small doses fear can be an effective tool. But in large, increasing doses, it does no good. Seek out HR or see it as a cue to flee to happier workplaces.

247.

Get sponsored.

If you're interested in being promoted or recognized with raises and bonuses, you need to have people in "the room where it happens." You need advocacy from people who know the value of your work and have a vested interest in your career success. A sponsor is not a mentor. They're an advocate. They might be your manager, sure. But more likely, senior leaders or your manager's peers. Cultivate those relationships and be transparent about your goals and aspirations. Once people know your career aspirations – and respect and value the work you do – they'll help you get there.

248.

Don't equivocate when defining action.

You've decided as a group that you need to take action. Be clear about the next steps and who's expected to do what. Instead of saying, "let's do XYZ next", "let's take that offline", or "we should talk to Bob first," be precise, unambiguous, and assign ownership. Some examples: "I'll schedule a call with Bob. Who else needs to be there?" or "This task will take a few days of effort. Jake, will you take that on?"

249.

Be the welcome wagon you wish you'd had.

When you get a new manager or colleague, roll out the welcome mat for them, just as you had (or hoped you had). Schedule an initial call to say hello, talk about what you do for the team, and how they can best contribute. Take early steps to build rapport. Get to know them as a person, and make sure they know they can turn to you anytime if they have questions or concerns.

250.

Ditch debt.

It can be tempting to "Keep up with the Joneses." But, when you spend beyond your means and accumulate debt, you add stress to your financial life. Try to set and maintain budgets, save more and spend less, pay off your credit card balances in full, and save for long-term major purchases. The resulting freedom from creditors will be worth the effort.

251.

Don't be afraid to draw.

You don't have to be a pro at using the latest and greatest white-boarding, sketch, or illustration app to convey your thoughts visually. You just need a pencil and some paper. We're not all the greatest artists, but we can all draw lines, squares, and circles. When you go analog with sketching, you can work more freely than you might be able to with a mouse and keyboard. Take a photo of your work so you can share it in a collaboration session. The next layer of sophistication is synchronous sketching using a tablet and stylus. This can be a really effective way to collaborate when you can't huddle around a white board on the wall.

252.

Use a habit tracking application.

You know how bad habits can become so ingrained that you can't break them, or even realize that they're a bad habit? You can do the same with beneficial habits, too. There are some great applications that motivate you to form and maintain good habits. And of course, you can use them to kick bad habits to the curb.

253.

HTH: TIL YMMV when u overuse acronyms.

Your industry, company, or team uses proprietary jargon and acronyms, right? Consider your audience when you use them. Is everyone up to speed? Let loose. Be aware if someone's new, or if you're speaking to an audience that won't understand the terms. Either explain jargon and acronyms the first time you use them or avoid them altogether.

254.

Cut out your background noise.

Life goes on around you every day. Lawn mowers, family members, loud pets, emergency vehicles, and delivery trucks can all impinge on an otherwise quiet day. When you're on a call, think about the effect those background noises can have on others. You can try to insulate yourself from noise intrusion by closing windows or doors. Or, use your mute button, noise-canceling earphones, or software like krisp.ai.

255.

Don't underestimate the power of likability.

Do you think your reputation as a good worker matters more than your likability? The latter may make more of a difference to your initial hiring and your continued success at work than you think. It's not necessarily a skill you're born with, either – you can learn it. Search your favorite learning platform for 'likability.' You may be surprised at how many options there are!

256.

Enlist others to help you find balance.

Other people can make a real difference in the balance you feel every day. If you find that days go by without having an in-person social interaction with another human, take steps to fix that. Seek out activities with people you'd enjoy being social with, start going, and open up and talk once you're there. Social interactions will follow … all it takes is time and commitment.

257.

Don't let "shoulds" command your day.

Ever feel like you should start a new project, buy the hottest new toy, or digest the latest must-read blog post, article, or book? It's seldom that you have to do something that immediate. Write it down first in a list. Come back to it later and see if it's still important to you. You'll find that most of what's on your list isn't that important anymore.

258.

Participate in communities.

Every day can look different for the modern worker. Every passing year brings with it new ways of working, new tools, and new challenges. The common thread through it all, though, is community. We can all share our successes and trials and learn from each other's experiences. Reach out to others through social media and purpose-built communities around the work you do. You might learn something, but more importantly, you might share something!

259.

Try walking meetings.

Is it nice out? Try a walking meeting. It could be a 1:1 with your manager or a small group meeting with no presentation materials. The audio-only nature of the meeting and stimulation from being outdoors can increase attentiveness and help ideas flow freely.

260.

Know when it's time to go.

You know the signs: you're feeling burned out, uninspired, or chronically stressed in your job. Your career trajectory has plateaued. You're not getting along with your boss. You're not passionate about your work anymore. Or, the culture has shifted to an uncomfortable place. Remember: you always have a choice: stay or go. If you decide to go, be deliberate, never burn a bridge, and use your network. Think about what you want and use your feelings to motivate change. You might have another opportunity waiting for you!

261.

You don't get if you don't ask.

If you want something, put together a plan to get it. If you don't plan, you can't act. If you don't act, you can't achieve. Ask yourself: what's the worst thing that'll happen if I ask for something I want? Very likely, the worst outcome is that the answer is no. Everything else is better than that, so go for it!

262.

Stick to the plan.

Reactionary bosses cultivate stressful environments. Be organized. Be visionary. Play the long game. Things go more smoothly if you have a well-publicized plan. If you're doing some of the following things, you'll end up leading a team with poor morale: ignoring or constantly shifting deadlines; having urgent unplanned meetings to resolve issues; tolerating last-minute changes without a strong governance process.

263.

Attend a conference or a meetup.

Can you attend an industry conference? You may need to travel but it's worth it to hear directly from speakers and mingle with like-minded guests. If you cannot attend, some conferences post some of their material online. Try a Meetup, too: they're smaller local gatherings of people focused on a specific topic. They're also a great way to meet people, build your network, and reinforce your industry knowledge.

264.

Don't leave follow-ups to chance.

Did you have a meeting where you made key decisions? Does someone need to follow up on the next steps? In the moment – or better yet, in advance – assign someone to document decisions and action items in a persistent place. Don't leave things to chance or rely on your memory. By being explicit about who's doing what and what decisions were reached, you'll avoid future confusion.

265.

Identify and mitigate distractions.

What distractions can derail your productivity when you're supposed to be working? They vary widely and can be rather unique, but the important thing is to identify them and take steps to mitigate them. Think about your phone, your tablet, your personal email, games, television, and other people nearby. They're all fair game to distract you and there are ways to mitigate their impact.

266.

Give your team the tools and environment they need to succeed.

You've set some great goals and targets for your team, right? Now, give them the tools they need to meet those expectations. These tools may be hardware-based (is anyone else's laptop in need of an upgrade?), software, or professional development. Regardless of the need, do your best to meet it to optimize your team's chances of success.

267.

Keep async async.

The only venues with rational expectations of synchronous communication are phone calls, video chats, or a scheduled meeting. When you ask for something in chat, email, or a collaboration tool, resist the temptation to expect an immediate response. Your message should be clear and concise. If you have a deadline in mind, cite that. Then, know that the recipient will respond at a time convenient for them.

268.

Take a break when the bathroom beckons.

Okay, this is about as uncomfortable as we get with these tips, but this is a topic that any remote worker will know well. If you must visit the loo when you're on a call, do so. But don't take your tech with you. Turn off your video and audio and take your break. If others will miss you, simply say, "Excuse me, I'll be right back," and turn off your video and audio. As a last resort, if you absolutely must not miss a word (really?) and you do take your tech with you, triple-check that your video is off and that you're muted.

269.

Limit work-related communications off-hours.

Avoid the temptation to be wholly available to your work regardless of the time of day. Mobile devices can make it easy to be "on the clock" in the early morning, late evening, and on the weekends. Try to disconnect, and know that the messages and emails you get off-hours will be there when you punch back in. Use "Do Not Disturb" or set app limits to ensure you get time away from notifications and emails that keep you in the work zone. If that fails, perhaps remove the applications altogether from your device. Balance this with any expectations of you being available for emergencies. If your team knows how to reach you by phone or text, that's a fine backup as long as you set expectations.

270.

Get wired.

Want to ensure that your network connection is consistently fast? Plug into Ethernet. Sure, Wi-Fi that conforms to newer standards is pretty fast. If you have access to an Ethernet cable connection you'll get right up to the maximum speed of your connection. Plus, file transfers, streaming, and backups between devices that are both hardwired will be far faster than Wi-Fi.

271.

Adopt a tone of neutrality.

There are a few devices that, when deployed in written or verbal venues, come off as non-neutral, accusatory, aloof, or even hostile. Avoid these turns of phrase: "as I said before", "as per my last email", "that's not my problem", and "you misunderstood me." Avoid formatting faux-pas: excessive punctuation (!!!), typing in ALL CAPS, premature escalation through the CC field, and excessive use of emoji or texting abbreviations.

272.

Be good to your employer; they'll be good to you.

You work on being visible when you're a distributed worker, right? Visibility is one of the key drivers of raises and promotion. Another is aligning your efforts to the organization's priorities. Don't just try to advance your own agenda. When you deliver against stated employer priorities, you communicate that you care about the enterprise as a whole.

273.

"Don't make me think"

When crafting an email, instant message, or any other kind of written async communication, keep this phrase in mind from the perspective of the recipient. Include proper context, relevant links, citations, or expectations around timing or deliverables. Recipients won't have to think as much! Clarity matters and can help reduce confusion. It's good to get it right the first time.

274.

Be truly present.

Imagine you're in a conference room with a group of people. The speaker is sitting right next to you, making eye contact and engaging with others around the table as they go through the agenda. Would you slouch in your chair, check your email, or send texts to your friends? No. Virtual is no different. When cameras are on (and sometimes when they're off), others know whether you're truly present.

275.

Step away from the tech.

It's good to disconnect periodically. Spend time away from your computer or devices each week. Go for a hike and leave it all behind, socialize with family or friends, or find a corner to read. You'll appreciate the focus you have when social media, texts, or work correspondence can't reach you. Give it a few hours and see how it goes. Get up to a full day and you'll be ninja-level.

276.

Create opportunities for socialization.

You have some great platforms for collaboration, right? Use them to create opportunities for your team to socialize with each other. Pose icebreaker questions in a synchronous setting or create a dedicated async channel aligned to hobbies. Frame the session so people know what to expect. The simplest recipe for a socially-oriented meeting is this: no shop talk, have fun!

277.

Give your people the opportunity to shine.

Your team works hard. Chances are, though, those outside your team don't know who those hard workers are. Give them a chance to promote themselves. Have them show their work to a broader group, take the lead on an initiative, drive a demonstration to senior leadership, or join a client-focused call. If that exposure is not something they're comfortable with, and they would like to become more adept at it, give them professional development opportunities to cultivate their presentation skills.

278.

Forget about the top of the hour.

Back-to-back meetings are no fun and can actually be quite stressful. Microsoft's Human Factors Lab conducted a study in 2021 that found short breaks between meetings can help alleviate that stress. A simple solution: start meetings five minutes after the hour or half-hour. This short break, built-in at the beginning of a meeting, gives you a chance to reset.

279.

Subscribe to podcasts for deeper insight and knowledge.

There are likely many podcasts in your industry. These are great for getting information first-hand from industry thought leaders. They can be a fantastic way to pass the time when you travel for errands or for work. You can listen to podcasts when you walk your dog, go for a stroll on your own, or during exercise.

280.

Make the most of travel.

For some people, travel presents more of an opportunity for networking than it does work. Try to meet senior managers and other colleagues you don't normally interact with. When you're remote you don't have random encounters with people in the hallway or kitchenette. Make the most of your physical time together and it'll pay dividends when you're apart.

281.

Don't micromanage.

Management is like conducting an orchestra. As the conductor, you should know the music (your goals) and the players (your team) inside and out. You should be able to point to a section (oboes, trumpets, percussion) and know what they're supposed to be doing. However, when a composition could be better, conductors don't abandon their perch. You don't see them rush into a section and start playing along (or worse, replacing a musician). Trust your team to do the right thing and give them the tools to do it. Trust, but verify. Yes, it's your responsibility to know what's going on. It's not your responsibility to micromanage, taking creative license and ownership away.

282.

Know when you're not needed.

Think you have to attend a meeting because it's on your calendar? Think again. This is especially true for recurring meetings where you're added as an optional attendee. You know the meetings where sometimes you're needed, but most of the time you're not? Skip them. Be transparent with the organizer, and make sure they know you're available if they need to call on you. When you schedule meetings, think about who's necessary and who's optional, indicating the distinction in the software if it supports it.

283.

Take action when someone is disengaged, disenfranchised, or underperforming.

Even if you're doing all the right things, management isn't all sunshine and roses. People will invariably have personal or professional issues that impact their work. See if they'll open up to you or human resources. There may be a way to help. Yet, there are times when rapport and communication will fail you. Teams are back when a manager allows someone to underperform. Choose action over inaction: address issues head-on within Human Resource guidelines.

284.

Form habits around things that bring you joy.

Discipline isn't just about avoiding things that suck productivity from your day. It's also about ensuring you do the things that enrich your life and bring you joy. Cultivate habits around wellness-related activities that relieve life's stresses and pressures. When you make fitness, music, reading, fellowship, learning, or a hobby a habit, it'll inject balance into your day.

285.

Soft skills and a growth mindset are critical to landing a job.

You might be a pro at using the latest software or tool. However, unless you can demonstrate solid soft skills (communication, problem-solving, collaboration) and a growth mindset (you can learn something new), you'll be at a disadvantage when it comes time to find a job. You'll be ahead of the pack if you can prove you're a quick study. Can you think on your feet? Do you know how to use your resources to solve problems? Can you learn on the job? That will set you apart.

286.

Single-task.

Multitasking as a productivity measure? It's a myth. When you try to switch between many tasks at the same time, you reduce productivity and amp up your stress. Instead, try single-tasking. You'll experience less frustration and stress when you commit to doing one thing – and doing it well – before you move on. Maintain an organized task list to help you stay on track.

287.

Never assume a person's pronouns.

When you incorrectly assume someone's pronouns, they can feel disrespected and excluded. It's even worse if you do it intentionally, or discount how important it is to do so. Encourage the use of proper pronouns. You might create an environment where it's routine to have this as part of your email signature where you work. When addressing a group, use a respectful gender-neutral salutation like y'all, everyone, or everybody – not "guys" or "you guys."

288.

Get involved with extracurricular activities.

Extracurricular activities can help reduce the isolation and loneliness you may feel. Office workers' strongest connections may be with colleagues. As a remote worker, your strongest connections are likely with people you see every day. Ask around: people you see all the time might know about activities you'd like, too! Talk about potential opportunities and see if something resonates with you. Then, make a bigger commitment by joining a group or volunteering your time.

289.

Plan and execute purposeful meetings.

You determined you actually need a meeting, which is the first crucial step. Now, make sure your invitation clearly outlines the agenda and what you plan to do. Ensure that all the key decision-makers can attend. Start on time. End on time. Capture key decisions in a persistent format. And if you conclude your agenda before time is up, end the meeting early.

290.

Start or end business interactions with casual conversation.

Take time to relate to each other as you would in person. It doesn't have to be a long conversation or derail the goal of the meeting. Is it Friday? Ask about weekend plans. See interesting art in someone's video background? Ask if there's a story. Opening the door with conversation can lead to a deeper connection.

291.

Remember what meetings are for.

Small group meetings are for collaboration, not "telling people things." Don't get your team together if it's not going to be collaborative. Company-wide town halls are another story, but if you need to communicate something to a smaller group, send an email or start an asynchronous chat instead.

292.

Give new things a chance.

There are so many different ways of working, managing, and leading. When you come across something new that you'd like to try, do so. You don't have to stick with it if it's not a good fit, but you'll be all the better for giving it a chance. There's nothing worse than an unyielding, unchanging culture, and relying on tradition is an impediment to improvement.

293.

Control your reaction.

You can't control other people. You can't.
What you can control is your reaction. That
includes whether you react at all! Your work
and personal life won't always be sunshine
and roses, and you'll have tough interactions
with other people along the way. Remember,
in the heat of the moment, that the only thing
you can truly control is your own reaction.

294.

Recognize the power of a skip level meeting.

One-on-one meetings with your manager are important. Meetings with more senior leaders can fulfill even broader goals. Use them to get more insight into the macro thinking that's driving your group's goals. Raise your own visibility by asking insightful questions and participating in the discussion. Use these opportunities to help senior leaders know you better.

295.

Try virtual coworking.

You don't always have to wait for something tactical to be on a video call with someone else. You might enjoy the feeling of being side-by-side with someone while simply working, mimicking the energy and proximity of a real coworking space. This type of interaction can help with single-tasking and focus. Give it a try at caveday.org, or try it on your collaboration platform of choice with someone you already work with.

296.

Trade video calls for audio calls.

Video calls can take a lot of energy from you. Try trading video for audio-only, especially if nobody is sharing their screen. Either turn off your camera or use the audio-only dial-in number if your meeting supports it. You can have more flexibility with an audio call and walk around, stretch, or do a light chore. You may find you're able to pay closer attention and have a more free-flowing conversation when you're not sitting at your desk, too.

297.

Practice patience.

Things rarely move as fast as you'd like. When you have to wait, recall the title of A. A. Milne's childhood classic, *"Be Patient, Pooh."* Information can make the waiting more bearable. If you're the one waiting, master the tactful soft inquiry about status (but don't pester). If others are waiting on you, set expectations and never leave people guessing.

298.

Accept praise.

When someone tells you you've done a good job, or have gone above and beyond, you might feel the tendency to dismiss the praise, deflect it, or minimize it. Don't do that. You're a solid worker, and when compliments come your way, accept them like an outfielder catching a pop fly. Confidently, yet humbly, say "thank you."

299.

Delegate.

You don't have to do everything yourself, especially as the manager of a distributed team. If someone on your team has a penchant for something that's on your plate, let them take the lead. If someone shows a willingness or eagerness to take on something new, give them a shot. To delegate is to empower, and empowerment feels good. Lastly, if you're struggling with something you don't know how to do, enlist a teammate to help to do the work. But, take the time to learn from what they do.

300.

Foster a diverse, equitable, and inclusive environment.

Distributed work is especially conducive to creating a culture of diversity, equity, and inclusion (DEI) but it takes work to get it right. Your company may not offer explicit benefits to nurture this culture, but as a manager, you can make it clear to your team that you're open to everyone's needs. We're all different but we strive to feel welcomed and valued in a group. Be open about supporting differences while embracing your core team's mission.

301.

Practice Pomodoro for productivity.

The Pomodoro technique can help you stay focused on a task and ensure you take periodic breaks. Developed by Francesco Cirillo in the late 1980s, the technique has you work on a task for 25 minutes and then take a 5-minute break. After four of these, take a longer break. Too rigid for your tastes? Try using a timer and vary the intervals to suit your schedule. The ultimate goal is to provide a focused environment to work on a single task during your best productivity time.

302.

Words and tone matter.

Think about the goal of your communication. Are you in the midst of a conflict? Are you communicating with someone who might take offense at what you have to say? Is persuasion your ultimate goal? The words you choose and the tone you deploy them with are critical to the effective delivery of your message. Think about how others might perceive what you're going to say. A gentle tone can keep others from becoming defensive.

303.

Normalize "I don't know."

Promote a culture where it's normal to speak up and say "I don't know." When you raise your hand and ask for the answer, chances are others have the exact same question.

304.

Don't just talk about the weather.

Conversations can't all be about the weather, fantasy football, or kids. Open up and talk with colleagues about topics outside of your daily responsibilities. It'll help strengthen and enrich those relationships. You'll be a better person and colleague by knowing who they are. What do they like? What are their fears? You'll realize that they, like you, are human. Keep your ears open and listen. You'll learn a lot.

305.

Gain knowledge from your network.

If you've worked on your own for any stretch of time, you'll recognize you're far better off when you can learn from others. Look for opportunities like conferences, workshops, virtual training, or one-on-one sessions. If you're on a team, create a space where you can share about interesting things related to your job or industry.

306.

Vote.

When you're working remotely, it's easy it is to use part of a day to handle medical or dental appointments. It's great to take care of that without having to sacrifice a whole day, or more than an hour or two. Same applies for voting. When it's Election Day, familiarize yourself with what's on the ballot and make a plan to vote. It's so important, and since you work remotely, it doesn't take a ton of time from your day.

307.

Create dedicated chat channels.

If your team is using a collaboration platform for asynchronous collaboration, great! Take it a step further and create dedicated channels to keep similar conversations together. You might align these to projects, themes, or broad initiatives. The important part is to get your team together to discuss and agree on an organization approach that'll work for everyone. One must-have channel: a casual one where you can share non-project things. It's fun to be social, but not distract from the focused discussions in other dedicated channels.

308.

Gaze into my eyes.

Have you ever talked with someone in person where they're not quite looking straight at you when you talk? It's awkward. The same thing can happen when you have a video meeting. Here's a solution: position your video window at the top center of your screen near your camera. Resize it small enough that when you're looking at it, it'll look like you're looking at your camera. It's a much more natural interaction for others if you're looking directly at the camera, and this is the next best thing. This approach is ideal for 1:1 meetings and interviews.

309.

Provide benefits to your entire team, not just those nearby.

Think about inclusiveness when it comes to remote members of your hybrid team. Going out for a team lunch? Do something similar for remote members and invite them to go out for lunch on you. Or, have your onsite team enjoy a lunch in the office and arrange to have similar fare delivered to your remote colleagues. Pizza parties for everyone!

310.

Advocate for your professional advancement.

Strive to grow and learn, regardless of your tenure. These opportunities are rarely given to you: you have to seek them out! I've rarely been turned down after asking for professional development opportunities. Employers are happy to learn that employees are thirsty for more knowledge. They'll have a more satisfied employee and you'll gain new skills you can apply on the job. Opportunities abound with online learning libraries, professional development, conferences, and seminars. Look around and see what you're interested in!

311.

Build rapport with your team.

You have to rely on voice, video, email, and chat since you're seldom face-to-face with your team. Use those technologies to establish some rapport. If possible, meet them in person sometime. It'll ease future interactions if you understand everyone's background. Professional encounters are more effective when you have more insight into their personalities. Talking about a shared experience, especially work-related, is a great way to strengthen a relationship.

312.

Measure your own key metrics.

It's important to measure things, whether you work for yourself or for a company. Peter Drucker said "you can't manage what you can't measure." Actually, you can't do a lot of things if you don't measure them. Keep track to help you plan your marketing, budgeting, and time management. At annual review time, remember that numbers and metrics mean everything to managers. If you're working for yourself, keeping track of key metrics can help you identify trends, too.

313.

Actively pay attention in meetings.

If you find yourself multitasking in a meeting, it's a good sign that you might not need to be there. Multitasking typically takes your focus away from the conversation. There's nothing worse than a huge lead-up to a question for you, and you're forced to say, "Oh, I'm sorry, I was multitasking." Don't be that person. If you must multitask, choose something that's not mentally taxing so you can remain attentive to the conversation. Try chair yoga, dynamic stretching, or another passive activity like working on a puzzle. You may find you're able to pay even better attention to the discussion and participate readily when needed.

314.

Don't be afraid to get synchronous.

It can seem easy to send that email or fire off a text instead of booking time with the recipient. Some conversations, however, are nuanced enough to require the synchronous touch. If you find yourself struggling with how to phrase something in writing, it's a good sign that it's probably best communicated synchronously. Get on the phone or start a video chat. Then, you can have a real-time exchange of ideas instead of hoping that your written message, as awkwardly-worded as it might be, lands where you want it to.

315.

Ditch the formatting.

You'll copy and paste things more than you do pretty much anything else on your computer. Learn the difference between the default paste and pasting without formatting. The former pastes what you copied along with fonts, colors, and more. The latter pastes text only, which can be invaluable when copying data from one application into another. It looks a lot more professional and is easier for the recipient when they don't receive a mishmash of formatting in their message. Are you a power user? Re-map the paste keyboard command to paste without formatting. It's easy to learn either the menu options or keyboard shortcuts for this, too. Search for "paste without formatting" for the latest advice online.

316.

Windows are wonderful.

It's nice to have a window in your workspace.
Natural light can elevate your mood, and it
can feel good to look outside during your
workday. When it's nice out, an open window
provides fresh air and ambient noise. For the
best results with videoconferencing, face the
natural light, or an angle from it. Never face
away from it.

317.

Create a communication covenant.

Agree as a group on where different types of communication happen and where you persist content. Email should play only a supporting role in communication. Important documentation should never be relegated to a local hard drive. It's far better to rely on asynchronous cloud-based approaches, since they encourage sharing, searching, and good access control. When you agree on tools and create habits using them, your team won't ever wonder where something is documented.

318.

Surround yourself with the right people.

If you've worked on a variety of teams, you'll understand it's not what you do that makes something special. It's who you're doing it with. People make the place. Look at the people around you, at work or at home. As Tim Ferriss says, "You are the average of the five people you most associate with." If you don't like those five people, you should make some changes until you do.

319.

Learn from the chameleon.

Every team has its own unique culture, language, and norms. When you join a team, notice how work gets done, how they collaborate, and how they organize themselves. There will be time to put your own unique stamp on the team (every individual makes a team stronger, after all) but first, seek to fit in and be a full participant.

320.

Know your purpose.

Do you feel like your work matters? Is it connected to your company's main goals? If you don't feel like your work has meaning, try to discover it through conversations with your manager. Ask how your work impacts the organization. Find out why what you do is important to your clients, customers, or visitors. You'll be far less likely to burn out when you're engaged in work you find meaningful.

321.

Don't drink during work hours.

Your work arrangement may allow for flexible working hours. If you're burning the midnight oil by yourself, it's probably harmless to enjoy an alcoholic beverage as a special treat. As a rule, though, don't drink and work. It may impair your ability to do an adequate job in the first place. It can also lead to all kinds of problems as you interact with others, synchronously or asynchronously. If you feel like you've had quite a day and need a drink to unwind, by all means, do so. Clock out first and then enjoy.

322.

Own up to your mistakes.

Did you make a mistake? Own up to it. Even if it's not 100% your fault, accept responsibility and take steps to ensure you don't repeat your mistake. After all, making mistakes is a very human thing, and learning from them makes us better.

323.

Focus on the individual, not just the work.

Your team meetings are a great place to focus on how the group is performing against their goals. They're the right place to share broad themes like enterprise-wide activities, strategy, and vision. When it comes time to check in individually, though, there's nothing like a 1:1 meeting. Don't focus solely on work. Focus on the individual. You'll learn things you can't in a group setting because we all act differently one-on-one. How are they feeling about their work? Career trajectory? Emotionally? By dialing into how they're doing as an individual, you'll get more insight and build a stronger relationship.

324.

Use your mute button like a pro.

You join remote meetings using your cell phone, computer, or another device that supports streaming audio. Regardless of what you use, learn how to use the mute button like a pro. Others shouldn't have to talk over your neighbor's leaf blower, kids yelling, dishes clanging, or (gasp) sounds from the bathroom. Don't we all have a story like that? Don't make that mistake.

325.

Make your smartphone a little less smart.

Our smartphones are so smart, they can vie for our attention all day long. Need to focus? Turn off notifications and place your phone face down or in a drawer while you're working. Better yet, use airplane mode. Minimizing notifications has a side benefit, too. By only having notifications for the apps you truly want to interrupt you, you free more of your time for other pursuits instead of checking your phone whenever it prompts you to.

326.

Use location as a productivity cue.

Want to get a task done without distractions from other things on your list? Move to another location, like another room or a coffee shop, and set a goal to complete the task before you get up again. When you change your surroundings in conjunction with a stated goal, you make it more likely you'll focus on that goal before you move again.

327.

Track your time.

If you're a solo practitioner, time tracking
may be one of the very first things you set up.
It's critical for billing, but keeping track of
your time may also shed light on
productivity-draining habits. RescueTime has
been mentioned several times in
conversations with other remote workers. It
tracks "time spent on applications and
websites, giving you an accurate picture of
your day." Apple devices provide usage
reports in Settings > Screen Time. You can set
scheduled downtime, limit usage, and
identify apps that take up most of your time.

328.

Get a chair you can bear.

There are so many options for sitting while working: a simple no-frills chair, office chair, executive chair, mesh chair, inflatable ball, kneeling chair, reclining chair, saddle chair … the list goes on! In short, you need a comfortable seat that gives you good support and promotes good posture. Test drive whatever you're considering and make sure features you need (armrests, adjustability, proper height adjustments, lumbar support) are all there.

329.

Be grateful.

Did someone go above and beyond in their professional responsibilities? Say thank you. If you get the opportunity, express this gratitude in a group setting. Public recognition can pay handsome dividends when the recipient feels seen and appreciated.

330.

Beware of office politics.

Look out for people who may take advantage
of you. Politics thrive in workplaces, no
matter the size or location. It's shrewd to
know people's motivations before entering a
negotiation, or before showing your hand.

331.

First impressions matter.

You never get a second chance to make a first impression. Don't squander the opportunity to let someone see who you really are. Do your best work, be your best self, and follow through on your commitments.

332.

Use inclusive language.

When you cannot see someone in person, it's easy to make assumptions about who they are. The problem with assumptions, and the ensuing language you use, is that it can put up relationship barriers. It can make people feel like they're not a part of the group. Inclusive language comes from not making assumptions about gender, race, personality, sexual orientation, or income levels. Inclusive communication takes practice, but it's worth it.

333.

"Want to see something cool?"

This question is the perfect segue to a quick "managing up" session. When you've done something share-worthy, start a conversation with your manager or peer this way. It may be a 5-minute collaboration, but the act of spontaneous sharing will generate excitement for your work. You'll get close-to-real-time feedback on your performance and others will keep you front of mind.

334.

Be charitable.

Giving is good for you. Whether you're giving your time, money, or goods, research has shown that charitable behavior results in happier moods. Create a goal for your annual charitable giving and enjoy identifying causes that mean the most to you. Gifts of time can also give you those feel-good vibes, so look for opportunities to volunteer in your local community.

335.

Keep your resume and portfolio up to date.

You may be happy in your job, but what happens when you find yourself in need of a new gig? Do you have materials like a resume or portfolio to showcase your work? Don't wait until the need is urgent. Set a reminder (annually is a decent frequency) to revisit these materials and keep them up to date with your latest accomplishments. Your future self will thank you!

336.

Master your own tech support.

It can seem overwhelming to be on your own with computers, printers, and networks that don't always behave. It's worth the time to learn enough about each one to do basic troubleshooting. Is the manual or user guide not helpful? Google the problem. If others are experiencing the same issue, they'll likely have written about the solution. When things really start acting glitchy, turn the misbehaving device off and on again. Lastly, make sure you have a network of people or companies you can rely on to help when things really go awry.

337.

Tell the truth.

There are many adages about truth, but my personal favorite is "Honesty is the best policy." Whether you've made a mistake, don't know the answer to a question, or feel like blaming someone else, tell the truth. Avoidance, evasion, and misdirection will cause you future grief. Lies build on themselves, so accept short-term pain over something far worse in the future.

338.

Remember that you're the captain.

You'll set so many courses in life. Your career. Where to live. How to invest your time. Choosing who you surround yourself with. If you find you have to course-correct during your journey, that's life. You're the captain of your ship, so your direction is ultimately up to you. You might need to consult and consider others (hello, family), but at the end of the day, make choices for yourself.

339.

Hydrate.

It's important to stay hydrated throughout your workday. When you're on your own, it can be hard to remember to get up periodically to stretch and grab a drink. Try keeping a big bottle of water at your desk. Coffee and tea (use moderation if you're affected by caffeine) are also fine choices. Try to avoid sugar-packed drinks, though, because they can mess with your energy levels.

340.

Ritualize your shutdown.

You don't have a commute to serve as a buffer between work and home, right? It's important to create a tangible transition between them because it's a shift of mode, not place. Put your computer to sleep or stow it somewhere if it's a laptop. You can even playfully say, "Good night, work!" Or, create a ritual around another buffer like an evening walk or a drink on the deck.

341.

Sleep your way to peak performance.

Want to keep your body and brain in top shape? Adequate sleep does wonders for your cardiovascular system, metabolism, and immune systems. Get enough sleep and you'll notice sharpened concentration, better energy, and an improved outlook. What's enough? The National Sleep Foundation advises that healthy adults get 7 to 9 hours of sleep.

342.

Take charge of your workday.

You're in charge of your workday. Stick to reliable start and end times and respect those boundaries. It'll give you space outside of work to recharge properly. It'll help your family and friends make plans with you, too.

343.

Raise your hand.

Do you see an opportunity to propose a new way of doing things? How about lending a hand at work with something that's outside of your core responsibilities? Raise your hand. When you volunteer, you communicate that you're a team player and have the group's best interests at heart. Plus, it just feels good to get involved.

344.

Beware of sunk costs.

Have you read about the sunk cost fallacy?
You fall victim to this when you keep doing
something simply because you've already
invested so much money, time, or effort.
There will be times when, despite your best
efforts, you'll always come up short. Read the
situation: know when to quit and when to
persist. Let practicality win the day and
beware of sunk costs.

345.

Seek understanding first.

Are you the type of person who shoots first and asks questions later? You're going to end up with a whole lot more injured colleagues and far fewer answers. Try to seek understanding without judgment first. Once you understand, judge away if it's warranted.

346.

If you want to retain the best people, treat your people the best.

As a manager, your biggest fear might be losing the talented people around you. Do what you can do treat your people as your greatest resource. They're not a commodity. Once you start treating them as cogs in a wheel, you've lost. Remember that we're all human, and manage accordingly. You'll know you're doing a solid job when your team sticks around for the long haul.

347.

Adjust your screen.

If you work with a screen all day long, are you sure it's properly placed? The top of the screen should be at or just below eye level. If you don't have a height-adjustable monitor, a few books can help you get there. It should be about 20 inches away from your eyes, about the length of your arm.

348.

Walk to and from work.

Well, other exercise counts, too. Since exercise has such great physical and psychological benefits, incorporate it into your day. You'd be spending some time commuting before and after work if you were going to a separate office, so why not use some of that bookend time to get some steps in? You may be starting and ending in the same place, but it's still a commute. Plus, that buffer time can provide nice mental separation from work and non-work modes.

349.

Assume positive intent.

When something impacts you negatively, it's natural to see the force behind the impact as having negative intentions. It can be so difficult to look instead for positive (or at least, neutral) intent. Seek first to understand the bigger picture and the broader situation. You might discover something that hadn't factored into your knee-jerk negative reaction. Of course, you may find that there indeed was negative intent, but that's going to be the exception, not the rule.

350.

Learn keyboard shortcuts.

Want to be even more efficient at your computer-based workflow? Learn the keyboard shortcuts for the applications you use most. Universal shortcuts, like Cut, Copy, and Paste are great places to start. Then move on to Open, Save, and Close. Once you realize how quickly you can do some things without relying on menus to find them, you'll never go back.

351.

Surround yourself with books you love.

Do you have some favorite titles that are go-to resources for your professional work? Keep them within arms reach of your desk, if only as a reminder of their value in keeping your skills sharp. Plus, you might have an odd amount of time before your next meeting. Use that to read a few pages of whatever you're into, whether it's a professional book or a breezy beach read.

352.

Max out your bandwidth.

Don't underestimate the value of good bandwidth from your work location. Nobody likes the Max Headroom-style stuttering that can come from poor bandwidth on a video call. Do what you can within your utility's constraints – and your fiscal appetite – to max out your bandwidth. Need to know what your bandwidth currently is? Search for 'bandwidth speed test' and give it a go.

353.

Don't mince words.

When you're following up on something, just ask. Instead of "I'm not sure if you received my email," try "I'm following up on my email." When you express doubt with the first phrasing, you make yourself sound insecure and hesitant. Be bold and don't mince words. Communicate with clarity and confidence, and balance it with tact.

354.

Prioritize self-care.

How can you take care of yourself better? If you think things like massage, acupuncture, yoga, or meditation are in the 'pampering' category, think again. These are not indulgent activities – no – they restore and rejuvenate you. Yoga and meditation are cheap or free. If you can, budget for massage or acupuncture and make them a part of your self-care routine, too.

355.

Get a decent webcam.

Post-2020, having a decent webcam is probably a must-have in your remote work tech arsenal. Sure, you can use your built-in laptop camera, but if you have an external monitor, it might be an awkward setup. After all, who likes the upward angle of a laptop webcam when you can enjoy the straight-on angle that a monitor-mounted webcam offers? Technology evolves fast, so look to sites like nytimes.com/wirecutter for the latest recommendations. You'll find many options with sharp video, great white balance, and efficient autofocus.

356.

Stand on a mat.

If you stand at all during the workday, try using an anti-fatigue mat. Studies show significant benefits to using them. They take the strain off your muscles, provide stability, reduce joint compression, and improve circulation. Your body will enjoy minor movements while you shift your position from side to side or front to back. Choose a highly-rated textured mat with contours that will get you moving while standing.

357.

Pay yourself first.

This popular personal finance phrase applies no matter where you work. Reserve a certain amount of every paycheck or invoice paid and apply it automatically to a specific goal. You'll be amazed at how quickly you can amass the money you need for your goal. Whether it's for a house, a car, or a vacation, it can be incredibly effective to reserve funds before you use them for routine or discretionary purposes. Bonus points if you do this via direct deposit, and the money never makes it into your normal accounts.

358.

Outsource your scheduling.

The process for setting up an appointment with someone can involve so much back and forth. If you find yourself spending copious amounts of time brokering a meeting time, try a service like calendly.com. With a few clicks, attendees can find and book a time, all within the parameters you set. Plus, they'll avoid conflicting with appointments you already have.

359.

Learn about the holidays and traditions that your peers enjoy.

You will work with all kinds of people from all over the world. We all enjoy significant events throughout the year inspired by religion, culture, or the countries in which we live. Learn about the importance of these events for those around you. Respect traditions and make accommodations for your colleagues to take part.

360.

Dress rehearse before the curtain goes up.

You wouldn't mount a musical or perform a play without a dress rehearsal, would you? For important meetings, get a small group of key stakeholders together. Rehearse the actual event using the same tools, applications, and talking points as the real deal. Make sure your screen resolution is good enough and that you know how to mute and unmute participants if needed. It can help to have a partner help moderate the meeting and chat while you're doing the presenting. This practice will sharpen the focus of your delivery, work out any kinks in the technology, and get invaluable feedback. Lastly, think through the things that can go wrong and have a contingency plan.

361.

Manage by results.

How are you measuring your team's output? If it's by the clock, or as we like to say, time with people in their seats, you're doing it wrong. Measure your team by their results. This is one of the biggest problems managers have when shifting to a remote work arrangement. They cannot see you, and therefore have no visual assurance that you're working. To be fair, in an office environment there's no guarantee you're actually working when you're sitting at your desk. How many in-office hours are spent socializing, online shopping, and scrolling through social? When you're leading a remote team, set the parameters you expect for results and measure those. How your team rises to the challenge is up to them.

362.

Run reconnaissance.

It can be easy to keep your head down and stay focused on your core mission. However, it's invaluable to poke your head up periodically and take stock of where you fit in the grander scheme. Proactively reach out to others. Learn about what they're working on, what their challenges are, and find out about their lives. This will help you counter feeling isolated or disconnected. You'll see how your work fits into a broader theme and direction, appreciate what others are doing, and see how your work connects with theirs.

363.

Tackle toxic presences.

If you have someone who's not a team player, misses deadlines, blames others for their mistakes and constantly gripes about everything, take action. You may fail, but try your best to turn around an underperforming team member. Too many teams are held back by a toxic presence on their team and the manager doesn't take action. It's best to address issues head-on within the constraints of what your Human Resources team allows.

364.

Remember: you're human.

The going will invariably get tough, and when it does, remind yourself that you're human. Humans make mistakes. Humans can get overwhelmed. Humans can feel slighted. And humans can be uncomfortable with change, uncertainty, and unknowns. When this happens, take a break. Turn off our computer and step away. Give yourself space and time to process, be vulnerable with someone you trust, and get back on your feet.

365.

Take time at the end of the road.

You finished a big project. It took tons of planning, coordination of many groups, and had its highs and lows. But you're done. And it's awesome! There's a saying: a new adventure awaits at the end of the road. Take some time before embarking on that new adventure. Relish in your accomplishment. Get some white space in your mind to think about what you learned and what you hope to get out of what comes next. New adventures beckon, but they'll wait for you to take a break to exhale, get some clarity, and reward yourself.

Scott Dawson

Index

Scott Dawson